REVOLTING JOKES for REVOLTING Kids

ILLUSTRATED BY DAVID MOSTYN

Ward Lock Limited · London

First published in Great Britain in 1987
by Ward Lock Limited, 8 Clifford Street
London W1X 1RB, an Egmont Company

Typeset by Columns of Reading
Printed and bound in Great Britain
by Collins

British Library Cataloguing in Publication Data

Smart Alec's revolting jokes for kids.
I. Alec, *Smart*
828′.91402 PZ8.7

ISBN 0–7063–6608–5

Smart Alec's

REVOLTING JOKES

What's a sick joke?
Something you musn't bring up in polite conversation.

What's the difference between a dead bee and a sick horse?
A dead bee is a bee deceased, a sick horse is a seedy beast.

What has four wheels and flies?
A council dustcart.

What has four legs and flies?
A dead dog.

'Waiter, waiter, there's a fly in my soup!'
'It's all right, sir, it wiped its feet on the bread roll.'

WATCH THIS SPACE –
AND START FROM
THE BACK

What goes ho, ho, ho, plop?
Santa Claus laughing his head off.

What's brown and steaming and comes out of Cowes?
The Isle of Wight ferry.

'Doctor, doctor, I've only got 50 seconds to live!'
'Come and sit down for a minute.'

Mother: What's the matter?
Little Jimmy: I'm bored.
Mother: Why don't you go and play football with Darren?
Little Jimmy: I'm tired of kicking him around.

What were Tarzan's last words?
'Who greased that vine?'

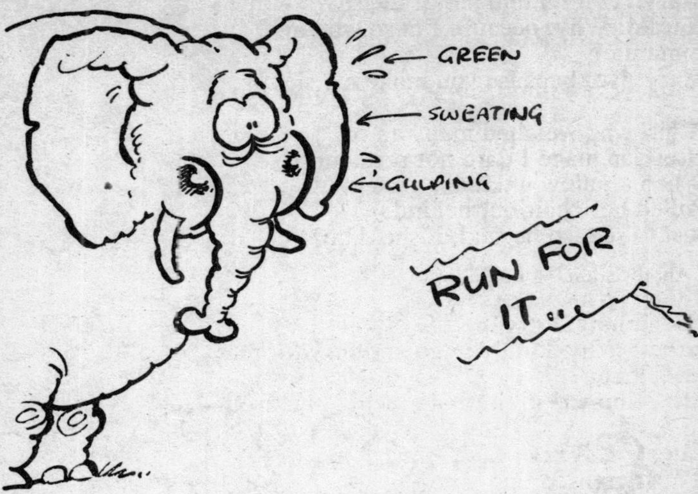

What do you give a seasick elephant?
Lots of room.

Which fish terrorises other fish?
Jack the Kipper.

What do you get if you cross a man-eating shark with a helicopter?
A heli-chopper.

Who invented vulgar fractions?
Henry the $\frac{1}{8}$.

Mary: You remind me of the sea.
Harold: Why, because I'm so wild and romantic?
Mary: No, because you make me sick.

A girl who weighed many an oz.*
Used language I dare not pronounce,
When a fellow unkind
Pulled her chair out behind,
Just to see, so he said, if she'd boz.

* Abbreviation for 'ounce'.

Why are cooks cruel?
Because they batter the fish, beat the eggs and whip the cream.

Freddie: Every day my dog and I go for a tramp in the woods.
Teddy: Does your dog enjoy it?
Freddie: Yes, but the tramp's getting a bit fed up.

Snooty lady in antiques shop: And I suppose you call that hideous picture an Old Master?
Shop assistant: No, madam, that's a mirror.

Why are sausages so bad-mannered?
They spit in the frying pan.

Lady in baker's shop: I found a fly in one of your currant buns yesterday.
Shop assistant: Well, bring it back and I'll exchange it for a currant.

If a buttercup is yellow, what colour is a hiccup?
Burple.

What did the absent-minded skunk say when the wind changed direction?
'It's all coming back to me now.'

What is an ig?
An Eskimo's house without a loo.

What do you get if you cross the Atlantic on the Titanic?
Halfway.

'Doctor, doctor, my baby's just swalled a fountain pen. What shall I do?'
'Use a pencil till I get there.'

What do you call those little white things in your head that bite?
Teeth.

Why do we have hands?
To stop our arms fraying at the ends.

Women in grocer's: I like your dog. It's a dachshund, isn't it?
Grocer: It is now. It was a whippet until it went through the bacon slicer.

What's another name for Dracula?
A pain in the neck.

Larry Jones was accident prone. He broke his ankle playing football, broke the dishes every time he washed up, slipped on a banana skin and broke his wrist. When he learned to drive everyone said it would be a recipe for disaster, and sure enough it was. He was involved in a terrible crash, which he did not survive. As he was entering the gates of heaven, St Peter noticed he had a large bump on his head, which was not caused by the motor accident. 'How did you get that bump on the head?' he asked.

'On the way up,' said Larry, 'I got hit by a jumbo jet.'

Sally: When is the zoo like an old carpet?
Smart Alec: When it gets a little bear (bare).

Bus passenger: Am I all right for the zoo?
Conductor: With your face, sir, you certainly are.

In the family's drinking well
Willie pushed his sister, Nell.
She's there yet, because it killed her.
Now we'll have to use a filter.

What's the most shocking city in the world?
Electri-city.

Why did the lobster blush?
Because the sea weed.

Knock, knock.
Who's there?
Sonia.
Sonia who?
Sonia shoe, I can smell it from here.

Did you hear about the man who crossed a budgie with a crocodile?
It bit off his arm and said, 'Who's a pretty boy, then?'

What do you get if you run the lawn-mower over the budgie?
Shredded tweet.

What do you get if you drop a piano down a mine shaft?
A flat miner.

Why can't a steam engine sit down?
Because it has a tender behind.

What do sailors say when they see a fat lady on a ship?
'A vast behind!'

What does one male centipede say to another male centipede when a lady centipede walks by?
'What a lovely pair of legs, pair of legs, pair of legs . . .'

Algy met a bear
The bear met Algy.
The bear was bulgy —
The bulge was Algy.

Hank: What would you do if you were camping in the Rockies, had just got out of bed, and met a bear before you had time to get dressed?
Karl: Run!
Hank: What, with a bear behind?

What do you call an American with a lavatory on his head?
John.

What do you call a woman with two lavatories on her head?
Lulu.

What do you get if you put floor cleaner down the lavatory?
Flash in the pan.

Why did the lettuce whistle?
Because it saw the salad dressing.

Two men were discussing their wedding days. Bill said, 'I shall never forget it. I got the most terrible fright.'
'Why, what happened?' asked Ben.
'Nothing,' replied Bill. 'I married her.'

Dim Dinsdale: How can you catch dandruff?
Smart Alec: Shake your head over a paper bag.

Careful Kate: What's the difference between head lice and nits?
Disgusting Dave: Head lice crunch more as you eat them.

'Your teeth are like the stars,' he said,
And pressed her hand so white.
He spoke the truth, for like the stars,
Her teeth came out at night.

What do you do with a lemon that's been mugged?
Give it lemonade.

What's brown and sounds like a bell?
Dung!

Newsflash: An elephant has been caught doing a ton on the M1. Police advise motorists to slow down and treat it as a roundabout.

What were the Chicago gangster's last words?
'Who put that violin in my violin case?'

First magician: What happened to that lady you used to saw in half?
Second magician: She's now living in Birmingham and Liverpool.

Barber: Were you wearing a red scarf when you came in?
Customer: No.
Barber: Oh dear, I must have cut your throat.

How do you find out where a flea has bitten you?
Start from scratch.

First cowboy: Did you know they called you Paleface on this reservation?
Second cowboy: No, why's that?
First cowboy: Because you've got a face like a bucket.

Mary: Is that perfume I smell?
Sheila: It is, and you do!

Doorman: I never forget a face but in your case I'll make an exception.

Where is Dracula's office in America?
In the Vampire State Building.

'Mummy, what's a vampire?'

'Shut up and drink your soup before it clots.'

'Mummy, Mummy, I don't want to go to Australia!'

'Shut up and keep swimming.'

'Mummy, Mummy, I've missed Daddy!'

'Then go and take another shot.'

In the small country town of Middlehampton Parva an inquest was being held on one of its leading citizens, Colonel Augustus James. The weeping widow had to sit down and rest several times during the proceedings, and it was with some misgivings that the coroner asked her gently, 'Mrs James, could you please tell the court what your husband's last words were?'

She sniffed loudly, blew her nose and replied, 'Yes. He said: "I really don't see how they can make a profit selling this corned beef at ten pence a tin." '

How do you keep flies out of the kitchen?
Put a bucket of manure in the lounge.

Knock, knock.
Who's there?
Moira.
Moira who?
Moira see you, moira hate you.

Mrs Smith: Doctor, doctor, my hair keeps falling out. Can you give me something to keep it in?
Doctor: Will this old carrier bag do?

Doctor: Did you drink your medicine after your bath?
Mrs Brown: After drinking the bath I didn't have room for the medicine.

Teacher: William, what is the Order of the Bath?
William: Mum, Dad, then me.

The number 93 bus was stuck in the rush-hour traffic, when a very large lady turned to the man sitting next to her and said in a loud voice: 'If you were a gentleman you'd stand up and let one of those women sit down.'

'And if you were a lady,' replied the man, 'you'd stand up and let all four of them sit down.'

How do you make a Swiss roll?

Push him off the top of an alp.

Jenny: How is a skunk different from a rabbit?
Benny: I don't know. How is a skunk different from a rabbit?
Jenny: It uses a cheaper deodorant.

Jimmy: I know a restaurant where we can eat dirt cheap.
Smart Alec: Who wants to eat dirt?

Radi was a circus lion,
Radi was a woman-hater.
Radi had a lady trainer —
Radiator.

Mr Parker: Waiter, can I have a steak like an old boot, a plateful of greasy chips and a cold, undercooked egg?
Waiter: I'm sorry, sir, but I couldn't possibly give you food like that.
Mr Parker: Why not? You did yesterday.

Irate customer: Waiter! This coffee tastes like mud!
Waiter: Well, sir, it was ground this morning.

Mrs Parker: Waiter! This lemonade is all cloudy.
Waiter: It's all right, madam, it's just the glass that's dirty.

Mr Smith: Our baby is the image of me.
Mrs Smith: I don't care as long as he's healthy.

From a women's magazine: The way to a man's heart might lie in the tricky art of cooking his liver.

Did you know that when the Queen belches she issues a royal pardon?

Did you hear about the cannibal whose favourite dinner was fish and chaps?

Bob: Rover's a very friendly dog. He'll eat off your hand.
Ollie: That's what I'm afraid of!

Queenie: This restaurant has no menu.
Rosie: How do you know what there is to eat then?
Queenie: You look at the tablecloths and guess.

'Waiter, waiter, your tie is in my soup!'
'Don't worry, sir, it won't shrink.'

Waiter: I have stewed liver, boiled tongue and frogs' legs.'
Customer: Don't tell me your troubles, get me a menu.

Where do vampires keep their money?
In blood banks.

Milly: Did you hear that Georgina has had her face lifted?
Mandy: Who'd want to steal an ugly mug like that?

What is black, floats on the sea and shouts 'Knickers!'?
Crude oil.

What is black, floats on the sea and whispers 'Underwear'?
Refined oil.

A proud mother telephoned a Sunday newspaper and announced that she had just given birth to sixteen children. It was a bad line, and the telephonist didn't quite catch the message. 'Would you repeat that?' she asked.

'Not if I can help it,' replied the mother.

Willie, with a taste for gore,
Nailed his sister to the door.
Mother said, with humour quaint,
'Willie, dear, don't spoil the paint'

Man: At last I've cured my son of biting his nails.
Neighbour: Really? How did you do that?
Man: I knocked all his teeth out.

Little Boy Blue: Baa, baa, black sheep, have you any wool?
Black sheep: What do you think this is, you twit, nylon?

Mother: Come in and have your tea, Ben. Are your feet dirty?
Ben: Yes, Mum, but I've got my shoes on.

First gardener: I used to work with thousands under me.
Second gardener: Really? Where?
First gardener: At the cemetery. I used to cut the grass.

Dave had been complaining about back seat drivers. Jim said, 'I've been driving all my life and never had a word of complaint from the back seat.'

'What kind of car do you drive?' asked Dave.

'A hearse!' replied Jim.

Annie: My father can play the piano by ear.
Brenda: That's nothing! My father fiddles with his bottom!'

Why wouldn't the piglets listen to their father?
Because he was such an old boar.

What were Batman and Robin called after they had been run over by a bus?
Flatman and Ribbon.

Motorist: I'm terribly sorry, but I've just run over your cat. Is there anything I can do for you?
Lady of the house: Can you catch mice?

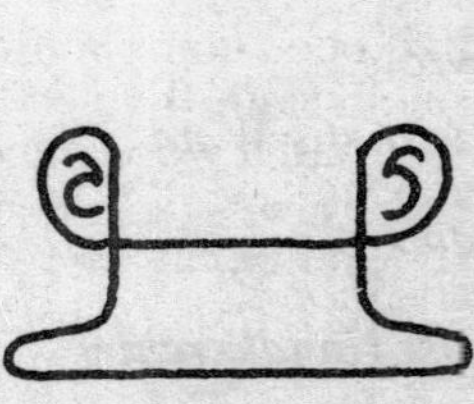

Mrs Jenkins: Whenever I'm down in the dumps I buy myself a new hat.
Mrs Jones: I've always wondered where you got them!

Jack: Do you feel like a cup of tea?
Jill: Oh, yes.
Jack: I thought so. You look sloppy, wet and hot!

Ben: Our dog is just like one of the family.
Ken: Really? Which one?

'When I was little people used to call me the wonder boy.'
'Why was that?'
'They used to look at me and wonder.'

Who wrote:

Gone with the Wind	By Karb
Padded Seating	Ivor Bigbum
Dracula	Pearce Nex
A Lousy Shot	Mr Completely
The Lost Handkerchief	Ivor Drippinose

Harold: Mike's given me his goat.
Mother: You can't keep it here. What about the smell?
Harold: That's all right, the goat won't mind.

What has twelve legs, six ears, a bad smell and one eye?
Three blind mice and half a rotten herring.

How do porcupines make love?
Very carefully.

At the no. 27 bus stop a man was eating fish and chips. A lady with a small dog joined the queue, and the dog got very interested in the chips. He kept jumping up at the man and yelping.

'Excuse me, madam,' said the man, 'do you mind if I throw your dog a bit?'

'Not at all,' replied the woman. So the man picked her dog up and threw it over the wall.

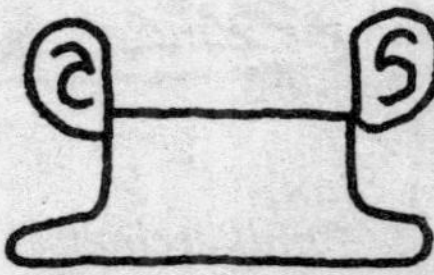

'Waiter, waiter, there's a fly in my soup.'
'That's not a fly, sir, that's the chef. The last customer was a witch-doctor.'

Why was a fence put round the graveyard?
Because people were dying to get in.

Did you hear about the two blood corpuscles who loved in vein?

What is a blood count?
Count Dracula.

Harry: Does your wife cook by gas or electricity?
Larry: I don't know, I've never tried to cook her.

If you lost four fingers as a result of an accident, what would you have?
No more piano lessons.

Peter: How can I get to hospital quickly?
Smart Alec: Stand in the middle of the road.

Bessie met a bus,
The bus met Bessie.
The bus was messy —
The mess was Bessie.

What do you get if you cross a louse and a rabbit?
Bugs Bunny.

'Waiter, this plate is wet.'
'That's the soup, sir.'

Clarence: I've been tracing my ancestors. I'm descended from royalty.
Lavinia: King Kong?

Who was Wyatt Burp?
The sheriff with a repeater.

What smells disgusting and shoots to kill?
A septic tank.

Who is short, swears all the time and is afraid of wolves?
Little Rude Riding Hood.

What did the lion say to his lioness as a Land Rover full of tourists drew up?
'Here comes meals on wheels.'

What goes peck, peck, bang?
A chicken in a minefield.

When Brian recovered consciousness after his road accident the doctor was waiting to speak to him. He said, 'I have some good news for you, and some bad news.'
Brian asked to be told the bad news first.
'Well, it's like this,' said the doctor. 'The bad news is that we've chopped both your feet off.'
'And the good news?' gulped Brian.
'The good news is that the man in the next bed wants to buy your boots.'

What kind of boats do vampires like?
Blood vessels.

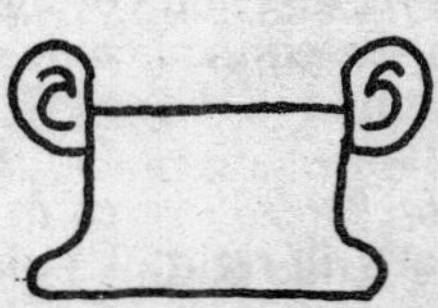

Rose's are red, Violet's are blue —
And mine are white!

Oh honey, you're a funny 'un,
With a face like a pickled onion.
A nose like a squashed tomato,
And teeth like green peas.

When we last had cottage pie for school dinner the council came round and condemned it.

'My chicken's covered in spots!'
'That's all right, it's only chickenpox.'

What's the best place to have a sick room at school?
Next to the canteen!

What's slimy and has eyeballs floating in it?
School tapioca pudding.

'Doctor, doctor, every time I drink a cup of coffee I get a pain in my right eye.'
'Try taking the spoon out of the cup first.'

What is round, red and rude?
Tomato sauce.

Sign in a grocer's shop: Will customers kindly refrain from sitting on the bacon slicer as we are getting a little behind in our orders.

Sign on Southend Pier: Don't throw
People below

Sign in a delicatessen: Our tongue sandwiches speak for themselves.

Sign in a Spanish hotel: In case of fire please warm the chambermaid.

Newsflash: Last night someone drilled a hole in the fence surrounding a nudist colony. Police are looking into it.

What are long, horny, black and smell of cheese?
Your toenails.

What's a skeleton?
Bones with people scraped off.

Little Milly was out walking with her granny. They had to cross a busy road, and granny dropped her purse, so they picked up all the money as quickly as they could and hurried to the other side. Gran looked back and said, 'Look, Milly, there's a pound coin in the road. I must go back and fetch it.' And just as she did so a huge lorry roared round a corner and flattened Gran. And Little Milly laughed and laughed and laughed — because she knew the coin in the road had only been a fivepence piece.

Young Sammy Watkins jumped out of bed;
He ran to his sister and cut off her head.
This gave his dear mother a great deal of pain;
She hopes that he never will do it again.

Mother (to child in tree): If you fall out and break both your legs don't come running to me!

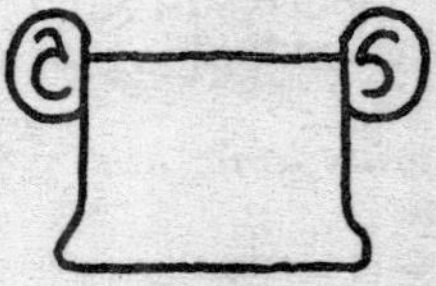

Mother: Why did you put that frog in your sister's bed?
Robin: Because I couldn't find a python.

Knock, knock.
Who's there?
Ice-cream.
Ice-cream who?
Ice-cream and cream and cream until I'm sick.

'Doctor, doctor, I think I need something for my liver.'

'Try a pound of onions.'

Passenger boarding aeroplane: How many times do planes like this crash?
Captain: Only once!

How can you tell if someone has a glass eye?
It comes out in the conversation.

'Doctor, doctor, is it true I haven't very long to live?'
'Let's just say that if I were you I wouldn't start reading any serials.'

What did the toothpaste say to the toothbrush?
'Squeeze my bottom and I'll meet you outside the tube.'

When does a bee fly with its back legs crossed?
When it's looking for a BP station.

Ringmaster: What was the name of that man who used to put his arm down the lion's throat?
Circus clown: I don't know, but they call him Lefty now.

Zoo manager: I'm afraid, Mr Brown, that your son is in trouble for feeding the baboons.
Mr Brown: What's wrong with that?
Zoo manager: He fed them to the lions.

What did Lady Hamilton say to Lord Nelson?
You're the one-eye care for.'

'Twas in a restaurant they met,
Romeo and Juliet,
He had no cash to pay the debt,
So Romeo'd while Juliet.

What do you do when your nose goes on strike?
Picket.

How do you get snuffly rock music?
From electric catarrh.

What did the spaghetti say to the tomato?
'That's enough of your sauce.'

What happened when Mary sat on a pin?
Mary rose.

Why do kangaroo mothers hate wet weather?
Because the children have to play inside.

Taxi driver: Haven't I seen you somewhere before?
Film star: Perhaps at the cinema?
Taxi driver: Could be. Where do you usually sit?

Smart Alec: Where do you bathe?
Outdoor Oswald: In the spring.
Smart Alec: I said where, not when.

Freda: I think Gloria's so good-looking. She has long blonde hair all down her back.
Flora: Pity it doesn't grow on her head.

Adam: You remind me of my favourite boxer.
Andy: Muhammed Ali?
Adam: No, I think he's called Rover.

Customer: A glass of water, please, waiter.
Waiter: To drink?
Customer: No, to practise my high-diving act.

Where do mummies swim?
In the Dead Sea.

What has five legs and two heads?
A horse and a one-legged rider.

What did the vampire say when he left the dentist?
'Fangs very much.'

What do you call a TV show about two comedians who can cure indigestion?
The Two Rennies.

What did the mouse say when his friend broke her front teeth?
'Hard cheese.'

What's yellow and smells of bananas?
Monkey puke.

A bird in the hand . . . does it on your wrist.

What would happen if pigs could fly?
We'd all need very large umbrellas.

History teacher: Why did Henry VIII have so many wives?
Smart Alec: Because he liked to chop and change.

'Doctor, doctor, I've broken my leg. What shall I do?
'Limp.'

'Will you love me when I'm old and ugly?'
'Yes, dear, of course I do.'

'Mummy, mummy, why can't we have a waste disposal unit?'
'Shut up and keep eating.'

Did you hear about the mother whose baby was so ugly she didn't push the pram, she pulled it?

Jane: My boyfriend says I look like an Italian dish.
Her brother: You do.
Jane, pleased: Really? Sophia Loren?
Her brother: No, macaroni cheese.

Theatrical agent: And what kind of bird impressions can you do?
Feathered Fred: I eat worms.

Glenda: Have your eyes ever been checked?
Brenda: No, they've always been brown.

What's green, round and smells?
Kermit's bottom.

'Is the leading lady good-looking?'
'Well, I wouldn't say she's ugly but she's got a perfect face for radio.'

Your brother is made upside down. His nose runs and his feet smell.

Why did the mother flea cry?
Because her children had gone to the dogs.

Did you hear the story about the dust-cart?
It was a load of old rubbish.

What's a vampire's favourite fruit?
A blood orange.

Bertie: What's another name for a coffin?
Smart Alec: A snuff-box.

Down the street his funeral goes
As sobs and wails diminish.
He died from drinking varnish —
He had a lovely finish.

'Mummy, mummy, why do I keep going round in circles?'
'Shut up, or I'll nail your other foot to the floor.'

What did Hank the hired hand say when his dog ran under a train?
'Doggone.'

What's a skeleton?
Someone who went on a diet and forgot to stop.

What does Dracula have at 10.30 every morning?
A coffin break.

What's a polygon?
A dead parrot.

What's the best way to cure acid indigestion?
Stop drinking acid.

Mavis: Clarice is an absolute angel.
Edna: Yes, you can tell by the way she harps on about things.

Jimmy: Mum, dad just fell off the roof!
Mother: I know, dear, I saw him go past the window.

JOKE FROM STARVING ARTIST.

WHITE HORSE WALKS INTO A BAR.
BARMAN LOOKS AT HORSE AND SAYS
'THERE'S A DRINK NAMED AFTER YOU.'
HORSE SAYS 'WHAT! - ERIC?'
HA-HA.

'Waiter, waiter, does the band play requests?'
'Yes, sir.'
'Then please ask them to play cards until I've finished eating.'

Daft definitions

Aperitif — a pair of dentures
Badminton — the reason the roast lamb tastes awful
Cistern — container for toilet water
Compos mentis — a rotting brain
Eureka — you don't smell too good
Faggot — a female maggot
Gangrene — an inexperienced team of workers
Hermit — a girl's hand
Humbug — an insect that's forgotten the words
Igloo — an Eskimo's lavatory
Living-room — a place you wouldn't be seen dead in
Magpie — pudding made from old periodicals
Margin — mother's favourite tipple
Oboe — an old tramp
Pas de deux — a father of twins
Presto — a tight shoe
Razor — get her out of bed
Shampoo — imitation poo
Son et lumière — your son's on fire
Touché — slightly barmy
Urchin — part of a woman's face
Urdu — what a woman has at the hairdresser's
Vixen — the vicar's son

Dad: Why have you got a black eye?
Willy: I hammered three fingers in the woodwork lesson.
Dad: That doesn't explain the black eye.
Willy: Oh yes it does. They weren't my fingers.

Harold: Why did you come home early from your holidays?
Horace: We were staying on a farm. The first day a sheep died and we had roast lamb for dinner. The second day a cow died and we had roast beef. The third day a sheepdog died and we had meat stew. The fourth day the farmer died and we left.

What did the man say when his doctor asked if he smoked?
'Of cough.'

Why is a graveyard so noisy?
Because of the coffin.

Mother: Don't look out of the window, Fenella, people will think it's Hallowe'en.

How do you make anti-freeze?
Hide her thermal underwear.

What did the baby skunk want to be when it grew up?
A big stinker.

Papa Moses killed a skunk.
Mama Moses cooked the skunk.
Baby Moses ate the skunk.
My, oh my, how they stunk.

There was an old man from Darjeeling,
Who boarded a bus bound for Ealing.
He read on the door:
'Please don't spit on the floor,'
So he stood up and spat on the ceiling.

Said one pigeon to another, 'There's the railway station. Let's fly over it and do a little train spotting.'

Did you know that the highest place in the world where you can go to the loo is at the top of Mount Everest?

Did you know that a famous nineteenth-century French painter had both an inside and an outside lavatory in his house? That's why he was called Toulouse Latrec.

The man who cleaned out the animal cages at the circus had spent all his money. He asked one of the midgets to lend him a fiver until pay day. 'I'd love to,' said the midget, 'but I'm a little short.'

Man, greeting wife: Hello, dear, I've brought a friend home for dinner.
Wife: You might have warned me. I've spent all afternoon preparing a stew.

Bert: You remind me of a film star.
Gert: Which one?
Bert: Lassie.

Everard: How are you feeling? You look a little pale.
Edgar: I'm not surprised. I nearly kicked the bucket.

What's the difference between a music maker and a corpse?
One composes, the other decomposes.

What did Lady Godiva's riding naked through Coventry do to her horse?
It made him shy.

Why was the Egyptian boy confused?
Because his daddy was a mummy.

Man at door: I've come to tune your piano.
Householder: But we didn't send for you.
Man at door: No, but your neighbours did.

'Waiter, waiter, there's a fly in my soup!'
'Don't worry, sir, the spider in the butter will catch it.'

Did you hear about the plastic surgeon?
He sat in front of the fire and melted.

'Doctor, doctor, nobody takes any notice of me!'
'Next!'

Annie: I think your Amy uses too much make-up.
Danny: Why?
Annie: It's so thick that for five minutes after she's stopped laughing her face is still smiling.

Sign in a hairdresser's: We curl up and dye for you.

Sign in a churchyard: Will anyone who has relatives buried here be so good as to keep them in good order.

Sign at a railway station: Toilets out of order. Please use platforms 5 and 6.

Carol: Your Eddie's full of himself, isn't he?
Monica: Yes, especially when he bites his nails.

Mother turkey to daughter: If father could see you now he'd turn over in his gravy.

Veronica: Do you love me?
Henry: I would die for you.
Veronica: You're always saying that but you never do it.

Why do traffic lights turn red?
You'd turn red if you had to stop and go in the middle of the street.

Why is your brother so small?
He's my half-brother.

What did the scales say to the fat woman?
'Go weigh!'

Little Willie, late one night,
Lit a stick of dynamite.
Don't you think he had a cheek?
It's been raining Willie for a week.

What do you do when two snails have a fight?
Leave them to slug it out.

Cannibal to his daughter: Now you are nearly old enough to be married we must start looking around for an edible bachelor.

Mrs Brown was always complaining about her husband. 'If things go on like this I'll have to leave him,' she moaned to Mrs Jenkins. 'Give him the soft soap treatment,' said Mrs Jenkins. 'I tried that,' replied Mrs Brown, 'it didn't work. He spotted it at the top of the stairs.'

'Doctor, doctor, I'm at death's door.'
Don't worry, Mr Jones, I'll pull you through.'

Knock, knock.
Who's there?
Nick.
Nick who?
Nick R. Elastic.

Knock, knock.
Who's there?
Donna.
Donna who?
Donna sit there, it's where the dog's just been.

Knock, knock.
Who's there?
Scott.
Scott who?
Scott nothing to do with you.

'Doctor, doctor, there's something wrong with my stomach.'

'If you keep your coat buttoned no one will notice.'

'Doctor, doctor, I've got double vision.'

'Shut one eye then.'

Little Miss Muffet
Sat on a tuffet
Eating her Irish stew.
Along came a spider
And sat down beside her,
And so she ate him up too.

Customer: Have you got pigs' trotters?
Butcher: No, it's just that my shoes are too tight.

Are two policemen a pair of navy blue (k)nickers?

I'm a girl guide dressed in blue,
These are the actions that I can do:
Salute to the captain, curtsey to the Queen,
Show my knickers to the football team.

What is sweet, covered in custard and bad-tempered?
Apple grumble.

First cannibal wife: I don't know what to make of my husband these days.
Second cannibal wife: How about a casserole?

What was the chiropodist's favourite song?
'There's no business like Toe Business.'

What do you call a man in a cemetery who's wearing two raincoats?
Max Bygraves.

'Doctor, doctor, what makes me flush so much?'
'Don't worry, it's just a normal chain reaction.'

Where does an undertaker do his work?
In the box office.

Tim and Jim were collecting conkers. They finished up in a graveyard, where there were some good chestnut trees, and decided to stay there to share out the conkers between them. No sooner had they started than two conkers rolled out of the bag towards the gate. 'Let's go back and get those later,' said Tim. 'We'll share out the others first.'

While they were doing this a little girl walked through the graveyard. To her horror she heard voices. 'That's one for you, this is one for me, that's one for you . . .' She ran as fast as she could, out of the graveyard and across the road to where she lived. Her mother was just coming out of the front door.

'Whatever's the matter, darling?' she asked. 'You look frightened.'

'Oh, mummy, come and listen,' she said, taking her mother back across the road to the graveyard's gateway. 'There are ghouls in there sharing out the corpses. Listen.'

Sure enough, as they stood there they heard a voice. 'That's one for you, this is one for me, and we mustn't forget those two by the gate.'

Did you know it is extremely difficult, even for a zoologist, to tell tapioca pudding from frogspawn?

'Bertram! Stop reaching across the table like that! Haven't you got a tongue in your head?'
Yes, Mum, but my arm is longer.'

Clever Clara: Did you know that a man is knocked down by a car every thirty minutes?
Smart Alec: He must be getting awfully tired of it.

Mr Smith to Mr Brown next door: What are you going to do with all that horse manure?
Mr Brown: Put it on my strawberries.
Mr Smith: Really? I always have cream on mine.

When are eyes not eyes?
When the wind makes them water.

Priscilla: Why do you put your hand to your mouth when you sneeze?
Uncle Peregrine: To catch my teeth.

Charlie: What do you clean your top teeth with?
Chloe: A toothbrush.
Charlie: What do you clean your bottom with?
Chloe: The same.
Charlie: Do you? I use paper.

Mabel: I'm reading a book called *Droopy Drawers*.
Ethel: Who wrote it?
Mabel: Lucy Lastic.

Young wife: I made two cakes for tea today. Would you like to take your pick?
Husband: No, I'll just use a hammer and chisel.

What do they call the cannibal who ate his mother's sister?
An aunt-eater.

What did one flea say to another flea?
'Shall we walk or take a dog?'

I know a dog as thin as a rail.
He's got fleas all over his tail.
Every time his tail goes flop,
The fleas on the bottom all hop to the top.

Should you stir your tea with your right hand or your left hand?
Neither. You should use a spoon.

A, B, C, Granny caught a flea,
She salted it and peppered it
And had it for her tea.

There was a young lady of Spain
Who was dreadfully sick on a train,
Not once, but again,
And again and again,
And again and again and again.

Magistrate: And why do you want a divorce, madam?
Woman: Because my husband smokes in bed.
Magistrate: But that's no reason for a divorce.
Woman: Yes it is. He smokes kippers.

'Waiter, waiter, there's a dead fly in my soup!'
'It's the hot water that kills them, sir.'

Mary: I've just swalled a bone.
Maureen: Are you choking?
Mary: No, I'm serious!

What tree can't you climb?
A lavatory.

Who wrote Rumbles Down Below*?*
M. T. Tummy.

Mrs Ramsbottom: I made a delicious stew for dinner but the dog ate it all.
Reggie Ramsbottom: Never mind, mum. Dad will buy us another dog.

'I never forget a face, but in your case I'll make an exception.'

Television will never take the place of newspapers. I mean, have you ever tried wrapping fish and chips in a television?

What's green and slimy and goes 'hith'?
A snake with a lisp.

Smart Alec: My dog's got no nose.
Silly Sue: How does he smell?
Smart Alec: Terrible!

What do you call a cat that limps, has fleas and is blind in one eye?
A catastrophe.

What do you do with a horse that has diarrhoea?
Take it to a horsepital.

Why wouldn't the piglets listen to their father?
Because he was an old boar (bore).

Mary ate jam, Mary ate jelly.
Mary went home with a pain in her —
Now don't be mistaken, don't be misled,
Mary went home with a pain in her head.

'Waiter, what do you call this soup?'
'It's bean soup, sir.'
'I don't care what it's been, what is it now?'

What do chiropodists eat for breakfast?
Corn-flakes.

Beans, beans, good for the heart,
The more you eat, the more you fart.
The more you fart, the better you feel,
So let's have beans at every meal.

How do you start a pudding race?
Sago.

How do you start a rude pudding race?
Sago to hell.

Mrs Jenkins: I'm afraid your son's spoiled.
Mrs Benkins: I don't think that's true.
Mrs Jenkins: I'm afraid it is. He's just been run over by an articulated lorry.

'What are you giving your brother for Christmas?'
'I'm not sure yet. I gave him chickenpox last year.'

Why does a tailor's son have a bad name?
Because he's the son of a sew-and-sew.

What do you get if a silly young goat falls into a food mixer?
A crazy, mixed-up kid.

Why did the typist have her fingers cut off?
So she could write shorthand.

Tilly: Have you ever had a hot, passionate, burning kiss?
Milly: I did once. Fred forget to take the cigarette out of his mouth.

Mary had a little lamb,
Her father shot it dead.
And now it goes to school with her
Between two hunks of bread.

'Your tights are all wrinkled.'
'But I'm not wearing any.'

Ken: I don't think my mother likes me.'
Len: Why's that?
Ken: She keeps wrapping up my sandwiches in a road map.

Len: I don't think either of my parents like me.
Ken: Why?
Len: When I got home from school yesterday I found they'd moved house.

What do you give a pig with pimples?
Oinkment.

Ollie: I was going to buy you a handkerchief for Christmas, Grandad.
Grandad: Why didn't you?
Ollie: I couldn't find one big enough for your nose.

Grandad: Last's night's dinner was awful. I hope tonight you're going to give me something I can get my teeth into.
Grandma: I certainly am. Here's a glass of water.

Rosalind: Do you think I'll lose my looks as I get older?
Victor: With a bit of luck, yes.

Clara: Our cat took first prize at the cage-bird show.
Sarah: How can a cat take a prize at a bird show?
Clara: He ate the champion canary!

Freda: I choose my own clothes.
Freddie: It seems to be the moth that chews mine.

Clever Clara: What do you get if you cross a skunk with a boomerang?
Smart Alec: A terrible smell you can't get rid of.

What dresses in long white robes and rushes through the desert carrying a bed-pan?
Florence of Arabia.

What do you get if someone hits you on the head with an axe?
A splitting headache.

A certain tribe lived in a remote part of the world where nothing grew, and where the only other living things were cobras and a tribe of midgets. Their diet consisted mainly of snake and pigmy pie.

Where do ships covered in boils go?
To the dock.

Said one egg to the other: But I don't want to be dropped into a pan of boiling water.
Said the second egg: You just wait till you get out. They bash your head in.

'Waiter, waiter, there's a worm on my plate!'
'That's your sausage, sir.'

Kevin: Grandad, can you impersonate a frog?
Grandad: No. Why do you ask?
Kevin: 'Cos Mum says we'll get £50,000 when you croak.

Inscription on the tomb of a hypochondriac: *I told you I was ill.*

Darren came home with two black eyes and a face covered in blood. His mother was horrified. 'You've been fighting,' she said. 'Who did this to you?'

'I don't know his name,' replied Darren. 'But I'd know him if I met him again. I've got half his left ear in my pocket.'

Nellie: Why does your brother play rugby so often?
Amy: Oh, he just does it for kicks.

There was an old woman of Clewer
Who was riding a bike when it threw her.
A butcher came by,
And said, 'Missus, don't cry,'
And fastened her on with a skewer.

Did you hear about the sword-swallower who swallowed an umbrella?

He wanted to put something away for a rainy day.

Who's the smelliest royal personage in the world?
King Pong.

Eddie: Does your brother still sleep-walk?
Freddie: Not since I covered the floor with tin tacks.

Lady Caroline: A tramp came up to me in the street and said he hadn't had a bite for days.
Clarissa Clump-Clogs: Whatever did you do?
Lady Caroline: I let Rover off the lead.

Should you eat crisps with your fingers?
No, fingers should be eaten separately.

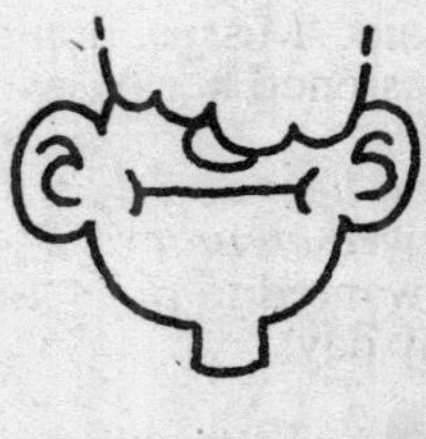

Mother: How did you get that splinter in your finger?
Tommy: I scratched my head.

Sally: Did you hear the joke about the dirty shirt?
Sidney: No.
Sally: That's one on you.

Who does a vampire marry?
The girl necks door.

What did the toothpaste say to the toothbrush?
'Give me a squeeze and I'll meet you outside the tube.'

What did the dog say when he sat on the sandpaper?
'Ruff!'

How do you make a Venetian blind?
Stick your finger in his eye.

How do you make a Maltese cross?
Stamp on his foot.

Samantha: I'm burning with love for you.
Gabriel: Don't make a fuel of yourself.

'Waiter, waiter, there's soap in this pudding!'
'That's to wash it down with, sir.'

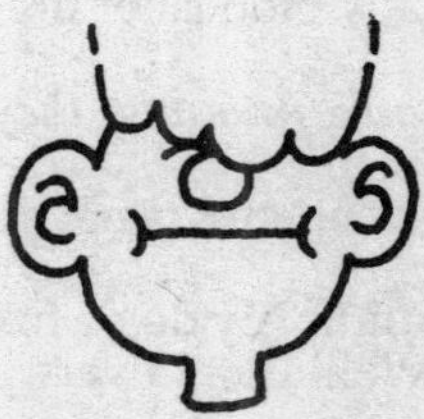

What does a fiend do at week-ends?
Takes his girl-fiend out.

'Waiter, why have you got your finger on my steak?'
'To stop it falling on the floor again, Madam.'

Lady in dress shop: I'd like a dress to match my eyes, please.
Shop assistant: I'm sorry, madam, we don't have any bloodshot dresses.

'Mummy, mummy, they say I look like a werewolf!'
'Shut up and comb your face!'

Mr Smith: My dog's full of ticks.
Vet: Well, don't overwind him.

'Waiter, was that cottage pie?'
'Yes, sir.'
'Well, fetch a dentist, I think I've just eaten a window.'

Simple Simon: I wonder how long someone can live without a brain?
Brighter Bertie: How old are you?

Mum: How did you get on with your first sex education lesson?
Malcolm: It was useless. We only did theory.

Policeman: Did you know that your wife fell out of your car a mile back?
Driver: What a relief! I thought I'd gone deaf!

Good King Wenceslas looked out
On the Feast of Stephen.
A snowball hit him on the snout,
Made it all uneven.
Brightly shone his conk that night,
And the pain was cruel,
Till a doctor came in sight
Riding on a mu-u-el.

What did the monster say when he saw Santa Claus?
'Yum, yum.'

'Waiter! Get that fly out of my soup! I wish to be alone.'

Why didn't the girl vampire like the boy vampire?
Because he had bat breath.

Where does a turkey go when it dies?
To oven.

Andrew: Since I met you I can't eat, I can't drink, I can't even sleep.
Annabel: Why not?
Andrew: 'Cos I've got no money left.

Patient: What should I take when I get that run-down feeling?
Doctor: The number of the car that hits you.

'Susie, why is your hand all bandaged up?'

'It's my boyfriend,' sniffed Susie. 'He held my hand, then he kissed it, then he bit two of my fingers off.'

Gloria: Why did you leave your job?
Glenda: Illness.
Gloria: I hope it isn't catching.
Glenda: I don't think so. My boss got sick of me.

Gilly: I bought this dress for a very low price.
Milly: You mean for a ridiculous figure?

Horace: That suit fits you like a glove.
Hugo: I'm glad you like it.
Horace: I don't. It sticks out in five place.

What did the lioness say to her cub who was chasing the missionary round the tree?
'How many times have I told you not to play with your food?'

First cannibal: We had burglars last week.
Visiting cannibal: Oh dear.
First cannibal: Yes, it was very expensive. And they don't taste as good as missionaries.

A cannibal bold of Penzance
Ate an uncle and two of his aunts,
A cow and a calf,
An ox and a half,
And now he can't fasten his pants.

'Mummy, mummy, daddy's going out!'
'Pour some more petrol on him, then.'

Willie in the cauldron fell,
See the grief on his mother's brow.
Mother loved her darling well —
Darling's quite hard-boiled by now.

What did the boy octopus say to the girl octopus?
I want to hold your hand, hand, hand, hand, hand, hand, hand, hand.'

What was the executioner busy writing in December?
His Christmas chopping list.

A motorist ran into a shop. 'Do you own a large black and white cat?' he asked. 'No,' replied the shopkeeper. 'Oh dear,' said the motorist, 'I must have run over a nun.'

Which rude saint is Santa Claus named after?
Saint Knickerless.

Ted: A funny thing happened to my mother in Manchester.
Ned: But I thought you were born in Plymouth.

Daft definition:

Nautical — behaving badly in a boat.

Mandy had a puppy on a lead. She met Sandy and said, 'I just got this puppy for my little brother.'

'Really?' said Sandy. 'Whoever did you find to make a swap like that?'

'My granny has one foot in the grate.'

'Don't you mean one foot in the grave?'

'No, she wants to be cremated.'

Why did the cow jump over the moon?

Because the farmer had cold hands.

What do you call a cow that gives no milk?

An udder failure.

'I don't like teacher.'

'Just eat the chips, then.'

Sign on the school gates: Wet paint. NB This is not an instruction.

'There's something about a farm that really gets you.'

'Especially when the wind's in the wrong direction.'

Want to sharpen up your appetite? Eat a packet of razor blades.

What do you get if you cross a man-eating tiger with a skunk?

A large striped animal that gasses you before it eats you.

'I've made the goose soup.'

'Thank goodness for that. For one awful moment I thought we had to eat it.'

'I looked up my wife's family tree. Half of her family were still living in it.'

'I used to be a werewolf, but I'm all right noooooowwwwwwwww!'

A man who bought a dog took it back, complaining that it made a mess all over the house. 'I thought you said it was house-trained,' he moaned.

'So it is,' said its previous owner. 'It won't go anywhere else.'

Surgeon: How's the patient, Nurse, after his heart operation?
Nurse: He seems well, Doctor, but there seems to be two heartbeats.
Surgeon: Bless my soul! I wondered what had happened to my watch!

What do surgeons do with their mistakes?
Bury them.

Does fast food make you sick quick?

Did you hear the rude version of Popeye? He told Olive to get stuffed!

What do you call rude Italian poetry?
Vice versa.

Smart Alec's favourite graffiti

Humpty Dumpty was pushed.

Today's pigs are tomorrow's bacon!

Say it with flowers — hit her over the head with a chrysanthemum.

Keep London tidy — eat a tourist a day.

Mind that child — aim for its mother.

Dyslexia rules, KO.

T. S. Eliot is an anagram of toilets.

A broken leg is not all it's cracked up to be.

Mickey Mouse is a rat.

Snoopy has fleas.

Frankenstein was lonely until he learned how to make friends.

Stop, look and listen — and be hit by a train.

Nobody loves me, everybody hates me;
I'm going to the garden to eat worms.
Long, thin, slimy ones, short, fat, fuzzy ones,
Ooey gooey ooey gooey worms.

The long, thin, slimy ones slip down easily,
The short, fat, fuzzy ones stick.
Nobody loves, everybody hates me,
I'm going to the garden to be sick.

'Did you hear about the eight idiots — Doh, Re, Fah, Soh, Lah, Ti, Doh?'

'That's only seven, what about Mi?'

'Oh, sorry, I'd forgotten about you.'

An apple a day keeps the doctor away. An onion a day keeps everyone away.

Prison warder: Do you have any last requests before we execute you?
Prisoner: I'd like to sing a song.
Prison warder: OK, go ahead.
Prisoner: There were 200,000 green bottles hanging on the wall.

Annie: Why is your dog looking at me like that?
Danny: Possibly because you're eating out of his bowl.

How do you start a flea race?
One, two, flea — go!

What time is it when you sit on a drawing-pin?
Spring time.

Dick: Is your sister pretty or ugly?
Rick: I'd say she was pretty ugly.

What is brown, flat and smelly, and goes round at $33\frac{1}{3}$ revolutions per minute?
A long-playing cow pat.

How do Irish dogs get bruises on their heads?
From chasing parked cars.

Why did the yachtsman have his left hand cut off?
So he could sail single-handed round the world.

Terry: What made you decide to become a parachutist?
Gerry: A plane with three engines on fire.

Nervous passenger: How far are we from land?
Ship's captain: About two miles.
Nervous passenger: Is that all? How wonderful! In which direction?
Ship's captain: Downwards.

A cannibal on a ship sat down to dinner and was offered the menu by a steward. He waved it away. 'No thanks,' he said. 'Just bring me the passenger list.'

What's worse than finding a worm in your apple?
Finding half a worm!

What's the best way to keep a skunk from smelling?
Cut its nose off.

Peter: What's a half-wit?
Smart Alec: Someone who's funny half the time.

Father: Kenneth! You eat like a pig. Do you know what a pig is?
Kenneth: Yes, Dad, a hog's son.

Father heard his children scream
So he pushed them in the stream,
Saying, as he drowned the third,
'Children should be seen, not heard!'

Darren: Can you lend me 10p? I want to phone a friend.
Smart Alec: Here's 20p. Phone all your friends.

'Do you know Fenella? She's got a face like a million dollars — green and wrinkled.'

When is a bird in the hand a nuisance?
When you want to pick your nose.

What is bright red and stupid?
A blood clot.

'Does this train stop at Waterloo?'
'If it doesn't there'll be an awful crash.'

Two girls were discussing a favourite film star. 'They say she's a lot older than she appears,' said Jane. 'Old?' said Janet, 'she's so old she knew Eve when Eve was Adam's rib.'

'If frozen water is iced water, what is frozen ink?'
'Iced ink.'
'I know you do.'

'Is that your face or are you wearing your hair back to front?'

'The baby just fell down a manhole. What shall I do?'
'Go and buy a book on raising children.'

What do they say about ghouls' parties?
'The morgue the merrier.'

Mary had a little clock,
She swallowed it one day.
And now she's taking Beecham's Pills
To pass the time away.

Why did Frankenstein's monster get indigestion?
He bolted his food.

Sharon: I feel as sick as a dog.
Mother: Go to bed and I'll call the vet.

What did one eye say to the other?
'There's something between us that smells.'

What does a vampire say when he's finished with his victim?
'Fangs very much.'

Did you hear about the boy who had diarrhoea and thought he was melting?

Tracey and Trisha were paddling at the seaside.
'Coo,' said Tracey, 'aren't your feet dirty?'
'Well,' replied Trisha, 'we didn't come last year.'

Doctor: I'm sorry to tell you, Mrs Feather, but I think you've got rabies.
Mrs Feather: Quick, give me a piece of paper and a pencil!
Doctor: Do you want to write your will?
Mrs Feather: No, I want to make a list of people to bite.

What's another name for a funeral parlour?
The departure lounge.

How do undertakers work out the cost of a funeral?
By dead reckoning.

Where does a ghoul comedian get his jokes from?
From a crypt writer.

What happened when the boy vampire met the girl vampire?
It was love at first bite.

Did you hear about the little girl who took her nose apart because she wanted to see what made it run?

Why did Humpty Dumpty have a great fall?
Because he'd had such a miserable summer.

Mother: Eggs are going up again.
Smart Alec: The chickens have lost all sense of direction.

How did the dentist become a brain surgeon?
His drill slipped.

How can you avoid dying?
By staying in the living-room.

Mrs Smith: My husband wants something electrical for Christmas.
Mrs Jones: Why not get him an electric chair?

Why did Dracula always carry his coffin around with him?
Because his life was at stake.

What is an undertaker's least favourite motto?
'Never say die.'

Attendant in the chamber of horrors: Could you please keep moving, Sir, we're stock-taking.

Apprehensive Bertha Bright
Wore her garters much too tight.
Now she walks about on stumps,
And comes downstairs in gruesome bumps.

What's the easiest way to get to heaven quickly?
Jump under an express train.

Smart Alec: I expected our new baby to be pink and white, but instead she's a horrible yeller.

Mother: Horace! Why did you drop the baby?
Horace: Granny said she was a lovely bouncing baby, and I wanted to see if she was right.

Father: Well, son, what would you like for your birthday?
Henry: Well, Dad, I've got my eye on a bike.
Father: You'd better keep your eye on it, because you'll never get your bottom on it!

What do you get if you cross a birthday cake with a tin of baked beans?
A cake that blows the candles out by itself.

Why do centipedes taste like chewing gum?
Because they're wrigglies.

'Why have you been sent home from school?'
'Because Tom Smith was smoking.'
'But if he was smoking why have they sent you home?'
'It was me that set him alight.'

Fred: Do you look in the mirror when you've washed your face?
Ted: No, I look in the towel!

Jennifer: Mummy, mummy, James has broken my doll!
Mother: How did he do that?
Jennifer: I hit him over the head with it.

Why do idiots eat water biscuits?
Because they're crackers.

Smart Alec: How old is your mother?
Jonathan: She's approaching thirty-five.
Smart Alec: From which direction?

Maureen: And after we'd been married a year or two, there was the patter of tiny feet.
Smart Alec: Was it a girl or a boy?
Maureen: Neither. It was mice.

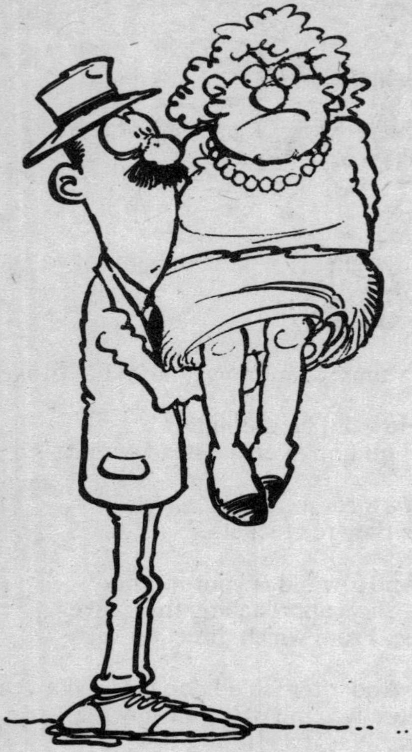

Father: Who is that at the door?
Jeremy: A man with a wooden leg.
Father: Tell him to hop it.

Mother: Who was that at the door?
Susan: Someone collecting for the Old Folks' Home.
Mother: Give them Grandma.

Notice in a barber's: Haircut for £2.50.
Children for £1.50.

Mr Brown: Doctor, I snore so loudly I wake myself up. What can I do?
Doctor: Sleep in another room.

'Doctor, doctor, I feel like a billard ball.'
'Get to the back of the queue.'

'Doctor, doctor, I feel like a pack of cards.'
'Shut up and I'll deal with you later.'

'Doctor, doctor, I feel like a pair of curtains.'
'Do pull yourself together.'

What do you get if you cross a parrot with a seagull?
A bird that makes a mess on your head and then says 'Sorry!'

As I sat under the apple tree
A birdie sent his love to me,
And as I wiped it from my eye,
I said, 'Thank goodness cows can't fly.'

What's the difference between the M25 and Terry Wogan?
You can turn off the M25.

English tourist in Paris: We've been here a week, Mabel, and we haven't visited the Louvre yet.
Mabel: I know. It must be the water.

'Mummy, mummy, may I go swimming?'
'Certainly not, there are sharks here.'
'But Daddy's swimming.'
'Yes, but he's insured.'

Did you hear about the woman who'd had so many face lifts that when she went for the next one they had to lower her body?

Mr Blenkinsop: Waiter! I have a complaint!'
Waiter: Well, don't tell me. This is a restaurant, not a hospital.

'My husband and I were happy for twenty-five years. Then we met.'

'Doctor, doctor, can you give me something for wind?'
'Here's a kite.'

What did they call the artist who specialised in nudes?
Bottichilli.

'Darling, how could I ever leave you?'
'By bus, car, plane, train . . . .'

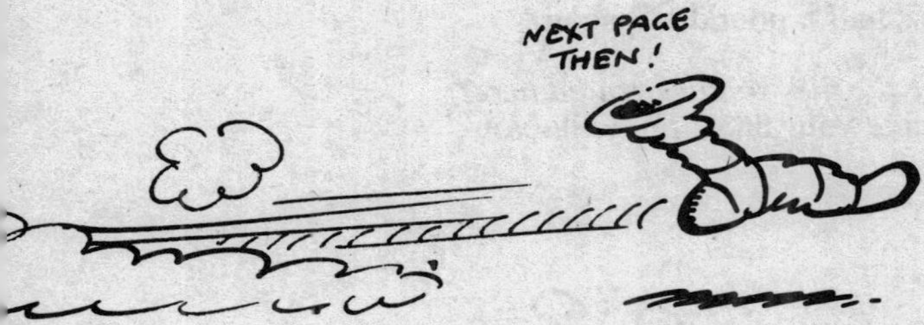

Gloria: Cyril told me last night he'd met the most beautiful girl in the world.
Marjorie: Oh dear, and I thought he was going to marry you.

What's green, has ten hands and flies a UFO?
A Martian suffering from air sickness.

What do you get if you cross an owl with a skunk?
A bird that smells and doesn't give a hoot.

'Doctor, doctor, can I have something for my kidneys?'
'Here's half a pound of bacon.'

'Why are the flies so thick round here?
'You like your flies brainy, do you?'

'Mummy, mummy, all the boys at school think I'm a girl.'

'What did you do?'

'I took off one of my high heels and threw it at them.'

Mr Brown: Why doesn't your wife wear lipstick?
Mr Shufflebottom: She can't keep her mouth still long enough to put it on.

Why was the frankfurter red?

It saw the salad dressing.

Mr Gibson: I think you just shot my wife.
Mr Williams: I'm very sorry, Sir. Here, have a crack at mine.

Our school dinners are so bad the dustbins have developed ulcers.

Knock, knock.
Who's there?
Dishwasher.
Dishwasher who?
Dishwashern't the way I shpoke before I had falsh teef!

Knock, knock.
Who's there?
Victor.
Victor who?
Victor his trousers and can't come out.

Mary had a little cow.
She fed it safety pins.
And every time she milked that cow,
The milk came out in tins.

Mrs Smith: Is it all right if I cook breakfast in my nightie?
Mr Smith: Yes, but it would be less messy if you did it in the frying pan.

Harry: I washed the budgie in detergent and it died.
Larry: You shouldn't have done that.
Harry: It wasn't the detergent that killed it. It wa the spin drier.

How do you join Dracula's fan club?
You send a note of your name, address, and blood group.

What game do cannibals play at parties?
Swallow my leader.

Was Richard the Lionheart the first ever transplant patient?

Sign at Smithfield Market: Do not feed the animals. They are dead.

If Batman is so clever, why does he wear his knickers outside his trousers?

What did the sadistic car that ran over an old lady say?
'I don't give a hoot.'

Graffito in a public lavatory:
Don't throw your fag ends in the loo,
You know it isn't right.
It makes them very soggy and
Impossible to light.

Man in posh shop: I'd like a fur coat for my wife, please.
Shop assistant: I'm sorry, sir, we don't do exchanges.

Cecil: Do you like my camel coat?
Smart Alec: No, it looks as if the camel's still inside it.

Are perfume manufacturers people who push their business into other people's noses?

Why were the tomatoes red?
Because the gardener told them rude stories.

Father: I'm afraid we've had to have Fido put to sleep.
Ricky: Was he mad?
Father: Well, he wasn't very pleased about it.

Cynthia: Do you know anyone who's been on the telly?
Sybil: My little brother did once, but he can use a potty now.

Sydney: Why does your dad take you to school?
Cyril: Because we're in the same class.

Invitation: The cremation of Sir Albert Higginbottom will take place at Hurstwood Crematorium at 10 a.m.
Reply: Put him on a low gas, I can't make it until 12.

Has the bottom fallen out of your world? Eat prunes, and the world will fall out of your bottom.

How can you avoid falling hairs?
By jumping out of the way.

Mother: What will you do when you're as big as your father?
Micky: Go on a diet.

What do you get if you cross a pig with a zebra?
Striped sausages.

A bird, a man, a loaded gun.
No bird. Dead man. Thy will be done.

Why is Camembert called two-handed cheese?
Because you eat it with one hand and hold your nose with the other.

Written in the dirt on a lorry:
Warning: under this dirt is a naked lorry.

Why did Frankenstein's monster give up boxing?
He didn't want to get his looks spoiled.

Which monster made friends with the three bears?
Ghouldilocks.

Where do monsters go on holiday?
Lake Erie.

Where do ghouls get their mail?
From a dead letterbox.

Who has fangs, wings, feathers and webbed feet?
Count Duckula.

What did the first vampire to see a pair of false teeth call them?
A new-fangled device.

Why is a vampire thin?
Because he eats necks to nothing.

What dance do vampires enjoy most?
The last vaults.

What's the best way to talk to a vampire?
Long distance.

An accident happened to my brother Jim
When somebody threw a tomato at him.
Tomatoes are juicy and don't hurt the skin —
But this one was specially packed in a tin.

Customer: Do you have pigs' trotters?
Butcher: Yes.
Customer: Well, if you keep your shoes on no one will notice.

Mrs Smith: Why did you divorce your husband?
Mrs Whitaker: Because he bit his nails in bed.
Mrs Smith: That doesn't sound too bad.
Mrs Whitaker: But they were six-inch steel ones. He's a carpenter.

A naughty child was irritating all the passengers on the flight from London to New York. At last one man could stand it no longer. 'Hey, kid,' he shouted, 'Why don't you go outside and play?'

How do you cure a headache?
Put your head through a window, and the pane will disappear.

How did little Liza swim a hundred metres in two seconds?
She went over a weir.

Lancelot: May I hold your hand?
Guinevere: No thanks, it isn't heavy.

There's nothing like riding a horse bareback for six hours to make a person feel better off.

'Mummy, mummy, why is Daddy running so fast?'

'Shut up and reload the gun.'

'My boyfriend is very polite. He always takes his shoes off before he puts his feet on the table.'

'Doctor, this is the second operating table you have wrecked this week. You must learn not to cut so deeply.'

How can you tell if it's raining?

Send your little sister outside and see if she comes in wet.

Mrs Rogers: But Phil, that isn't our baby!
Mr Rogers: I know, but it's a much more expensive pram.

An apple a day keeps the doctor away — if you aim it well.

Salesman: Does your husband have a life insurance policy?
Wife: No, just fire insurance. He knows where he's going.

Silly Sue: We bumped into some old friends last week.
Smart Alec: Your brother was driving again, was he?

Barrister: Can you explain why you stabbed your wife 67 times?
Man: I couldn't switch off the electric carving knife.

What's the best way to avoid catching diseases from biting insects?
Stop biting them.

Minerva: Did you miss me while I was away?
Martin: Were you away?

Betty: Who's that red-haired woman with the wart?
Letty: Shh, that's her husband.

More favourite graffiti:

This is the age of the train.
Ours was 194.

Just gone for a walk round the block.
(signed) Anne Boleyn

Punk is dead
It certainly smells as if it is.

Watership Down
You've read the book
You've seen the film
— Now eat the pie!

Mrs Jenkins: What's your mother-in-law like?
Mrs Jones: Well, I wouldn't say she was mean, but she keeps a fork in the sugar basin.

Customer: Why is my pie all squashed?
Waiter: Well, you did ask me to step on it.

What's a mushroom?
The school dining hall.

Sign in a cafe: Don't complain about the tea. You'll be old and weak yourself one day.

Sign in a lavatory: In the interests of economy please use both sides of the paper.

What happens when plumbers die?
They go down the drain.

What's the name for a short-legged tramp?
A low-down bum.

There was a strange fellow of Tyre
Who constantly sat on the fire.
When asked, 'Are you hot?'
He said, 'Certainly not,
I'm James Winterbottom, Esq.'

There was a young lady called Rose,
Who had a large wart on her nose.
When she had it removed,
Her appearance improved,
But her glasses slipped down to her toes.

What did one candle say to another?
'You're getting on my wick.'

Patient: Doctor, doctor, I feel half dead.
Doctor: I'll arrange for you to be buried from the waist down.

Did you hear the one abut the two fat men who ran in a race? One ran in short bursts, the other ran in burst shorts.

Nurse in hospital: Does your wife miss you a lot?
Patient in bed: No, she's a good shot. That's why I'm in here.

Why did the cannibal feel sick every time he'd eaten a missionary?
Because you can't keep a good man down.

Do you know why the human race is so confused? Adam was Eve's mother!

What did Adam do when he met Eve?
Turned over a new leaf!

Why wasn't Eve afraid of catching measles?
Because she'd Adam.

Sharon: Why did you chuck away your new boyfriend?
Sheila: He had a mind like a Welsh railway.
Sharon: What do you mean?
Sheila: One track and dirty.

'I managed to stop my son biting his nails.'
How did you do that?'
'I bought him some shoes.'

Science teacher: What is water, Cuthbert?
Cuthbert: It's a colourless liquid that turns black when I put my hands in it.

Sign in a German lavatory: Now wash your Hans.

Did you hear that the royal family in Holland were all ill? They've got Dutch Realm Disease.

When the cow fell over the cliff little Sarah couldn't stop laughing. You see, she knew there was no point in crying over spilt milk.

Mother: Have you put the cat out, dear?
Father: I think I must have. I just trod on his tail.

What's the best cure for dandruff?
Going bald.

What is old, pink and wrinkled, and belongs to Grandma?
Grandpa.

What had fifty legs but cannot walk?
Half a centipede.

Woman in delicatessen: Who's serving nuts?
Assistant: I'll be with you in a minute, madam.

What makes you think a surgeon hates people?
He's always sticking his knife into them.

Why did the man have a high-pitched voice and teeth that moved up and down?
Because he had a falsetto voice and a false set o' teeth.

What did the germ say to the virus?
Don't bacilli.

Mother: Miranda, why are you making faces at that warthog?
Miranda: He started it!

Which northern town sells meat that makes you ill?
Oldham.

Tracey: I think I've just swallowed a fly.
Terry: Shouldn't you take something for it?
Tracey: No, I think I'll just let it starve.

'I don't think my parents like me very much. When I asked them for a cuddly pet they bought me a piranha fish.'

Why did the undertaker's assistant want to change his job?
He thought it was a dead-end occupation.

What is small, spotty and deadly?
A lady bird with a machine gun.

'Doctor, how can I stop my nose running?'
'Stick out your foot and trip it up.'

Darren (at the theatre): Do you have a good seat?
Doris: Yes, thank you.
Darren: You can see all right?
Doris: Yes, fine thanks.
Darren: There's nobody blocking your view?
Doris: No.
Darren: Are you sure?
Doris: Yes, quite sure.
Darren: Will you change places with me, then?

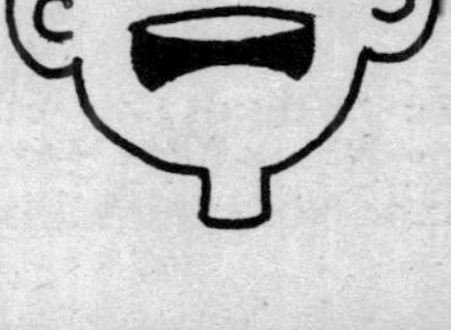

Mother: I was hoping you'd be kind to little Michael and let him have the last piece of cake. Look at the way the mother blackbird gives all the best bits of food to her babies.
Millicent: I'd do that too if I had to eat worms.

Why are members of a vampire's family so close to each other?
Because blood's thicker than water.

There was a young lady of Riga,
Who rode, with a smile, on a tiger;
They returned from the ride
With the lady inside,
And the smile on the face of the tiger.

There was a young lady from Twickenham
Whose boots were too tight to walk quick in 'em.
She bore them awhile,
Then stopped at a stile,
And took them both off and was sick in 'em.

What's a dirty postcard?
One the postman has dropped in the mud.

'Now Jenny, tell me where you buried Daddy. He's got the car keys in his pocket.'

What could the waiter at the vampires' restaurant never serve?
Steak (stake).

If a famous murderer was born in Afghanistan, grew up in Australia, spent ten years shooting people in America and then came to Britain and died, what would he be?
Dead.

What did the skeleton say when the lady came round with a collecting box?
'Sorry, I'm skint.'

A small, thin, weedy little man went into a pub for a drink. He was fascinated by the barmaid, who was going bald, had droopy, bloodshot eyes, and was altogether extremely ugly. He turned to the man next to him and said, 'What an amazing-looking barmaid.'

The man got hold of his coat collar and snarled, 'That barmaid is my sister.'

'Goodness,' said the weedy little man. 'Doesn't her face suit her!'

Why did the two cyclops fight?
Because they could never see eye to eye over anything.

If it takes an apple a day to keep the doctor away, how many does it take to get rid of the nurse?

'Doctor, doctor, I feel like a yo-yo.'
'Sit down, sit down, sit down.'

Mother: Now you have finished your supper, you must say grace.
Jimmy: Thanks for the grub, God.
Mother: That wasn't a very nice grace, Jimmy.
Jimmy: It wasn't a very nice supper, either.

Two old friends met, twenty years after the last war. One said to the other, 'Is that your face or are you still wearing a gas mask?'

Mr Smith: Didn't you hear my hammering on your wall during your party last night?
Mr Jones: That's all right. We were making quite a lot of noise ourselves.

Science teacher: Now my hat, here, represents the moon. Any questions?
Clarence: Yes, sir. Is the moon inhabited?

How can you kill a Scotsman with a £1 coin?
Throw it under a bus.

Man in restaurant: Do you mind me smoking?
Fellow diner: Not if you don't mind me being sick.

A beggar knocked at the door of a house and asked for food. 'Didn't I give you some dinner last week?' enquired the householder suspiciously.

'Yes,' replied the beggar, 'but I'm quite well again now.'

Davie: Mum, I've just knocked over that ladder at the side of the house.
Mother: You'd better go and tell your father.
Davie: He knows already. He was at the top of it when I knocked it over.

Elderly Aunt Prudence lived for many years with Jim and Julie Jeremiah. She was a bad-tempered old woman, and when she eventually died the couple felt a great sense of relief. 'Dearest,' said Jim, 'I don't want to be nasty, but I don't think I could have lived with your Aunt Prudence for many more years.'

'My Aunt Prudence!' exclaimed Julie, 'I always thought she was your Aunt Prudence!'

Did you hear about the girl who was so ugly that at Christmas the boys hung her up and kissed the mistletoe?

First Housewife: I always shop at Bigginton's. They have such lovely warm pies.
Second Housewife: That's because the cat sits on them all day.

Smart Alec: Who wrote *The Vicious Hungry Lion*?
Dim Dinsdale: I don't know. Who wrote *The Vicious Hungry Lion*?
Smart Alec: Claudia Handoff.

There was once an old man called Keith,
Who mislaid his set of false teeth.
Laid them on a chair,
Forget they were there,
Sat down, and was bitten beneath.

Knock, knock.
Who's there?
Tom.
Tom who?
Tom Orrow I'll get even with you, just you wait and see!

What did one skunk say to another when they met?

'Let us spray.'

'Doctor, doctor, my mother-in-law's just dislocated her jaw. Could you come and see her in about six months?'

Why did the old lady blush as she walked past the hen coop?

Because she heard foul (fowl) language.

Waiter: We have almost everything on the menu, sir.
Diner: So I see. Could I have a clean one, please?

Henry: How dare you tell everyone I'm a stupid old fool!
Horace: Sorry, I didn't know it was a secret.

Cannibal mother to her son: How many times have I told you not to speak when you've got someone in your mouth?

The village idiot sat on the side of the road with a fishing line down the drain. Feeling sorry for him, and wanting to humour him, a lady gave him 50p and asked kindly, 'How many have you caught?'
'You're the tenth this morning,' was the reply.

What did the girl watch say to the boy watch?
'Keep your hands to yourself.'

Indignant middle-aged woman: I've got the face of a sixteen-year-old!
Her husband: Well give it back, you're wearing it out.

Advertisement: Keep that schoolgirl complexion . . .
Smart Alec: All the schoolgirls I know have spots.

Diner: Waiter! This food is dreadful! Bring me the manager!
Waiter: He won't taste any better, sir.

Bill: My father died last Sunday lunch-time.
Ben: How dreadful! What happened?
Bill: He went down to the garden to pick some beans for lunch, fell over, and died.
Ben: Whatever did your mother do?
Bill: What could she do? She opened a packet of frozen peas.

'Doctor, doctor, I keep pulling ugly faces.'
'Don't worry, people won't notice anything unusual.'

Sam, Sam, the dirty man,
Washed his face in the frying pan,
Combed his hair with a donkey's tail,
And scratched his belly with his big toenail.

STAN PIPES OF MOTHERWELL, SENT US THIS WELL CONSIDERED DRAWING OF ONE OF HIS TOENAILS.

THANKS STAN, AND KEEP CLIPPING SAYS OUR EDITOR.

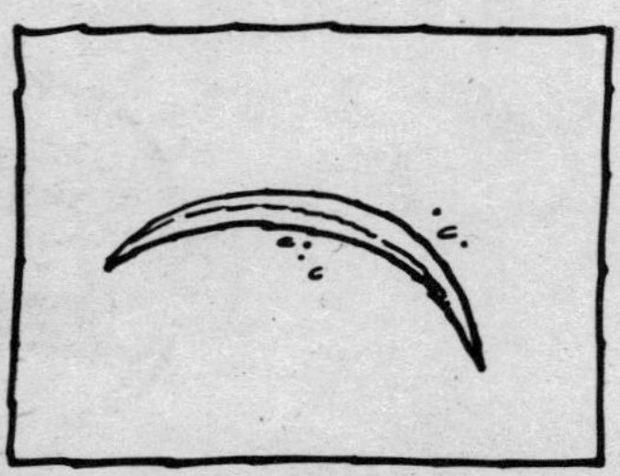

Knock, knock.
Who's there?
Bo.
Bo who?
Bogies up your nose.

Knock, knock.
Who's there?
Pooh.
Pooh who?
Pooh, what an awful smell!

The boy stood on the burning deck
Picking his nose like mad.
He rolled it into little balls,
And threw them at his Dad.

Lady customer: I didn't come here to be insulted!
Shop assistant: Where do you usually go?

'I heard you buried your Granny last week.'
'We had to. She was dead.'

How can you stop a cold going to your chest?
Tie a knot in your neck.

What happened on the farm when the milking machine fused?
Udder chaos.

A man walked into a Glasgow bar. 'Do you serve Sassenachs?' he asked.
'Certainly, sir,' replied the barman.
'A pint of bitter for me, and a couple of Sassenachs for my Alsatian, please.'

'Our parrot lays square eggs.'
'Good heavens! Can it talk, too?'
'Yes, but it only says one word.'
'What's that?'
'Ouch!'

What kind of necklace does a lady ghoul wear?
One made of tomb stones.

A man who had a terrible accident woke up in hospital with his face all covered in bandages. The doctor said, 'You'll be glad to hear we managed to save your eye, even though the rest of you is a bit of a mess.'

'That's wonderful,' said the patient.

'Yes,' replied the surgeon. 'We'll give it to you as a memento when you go home.'

'Waiter, waiter, there's a button in my salad.'
'It must have come off a jacket potato, sir.'

Rude boy: What's the difference between dog dirt and chocolate?
Dim girl: I don't know.
Rude boy: I'm not sending you out to buy my chocolates, then!

Here I sit all alone in the moonlight,
Abandoned by women and men,
Muttering, over and over,
'I'll never eat garlic again!'

A man coughed violently, and his false teeth shot across the room and smashed against the wall. 'Oh dear,' he said, 'whatever shall I do? I can't afford a new set.'

'Don't worry,' said his friend. 'I'll get a pair from my brother for you.'

The next day the friend came back with the teeth, which fitted perfectly. 'This is wonderful,' said the man. 'Your brother must be a very good dentist.'

'Oh, he's not a dentist,' replied his friend. 'He's an undertaker.'

How can you tell when Grandpa is hiding in the oven?

You can't shut the door.

Two men had just finished laying a fitted carpet when they noticed a small lump in the centre of it. 'Must be my packet of wine gums,' said one. 'I wondered where I'd dropped them.' So he took a large hammer and squashed the lump flat, rather than taking up the carpet again.

At that moment the owner of the house came in, carrying something in her hand. 'Did either of you leave a packet of wine gums in the kitchen?' she asked. 'And I don't suppose you've seen my son's white mouse, have you? He seems to have escaped.'

What did one virus say to another?

'Stay away, I think I've got penicillin.'

Hooray Henry: Who wrote *My Life of Crime*?
Smart Alec: Robin Banks.

Diner: How much is lunch at this restaurant?
Manager: £15 a head, sir.
Diner: Just bring me an ear, then.

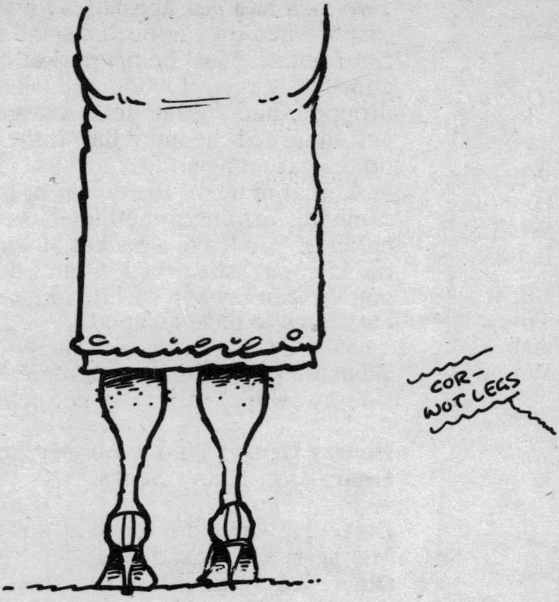

First diner: The fish in this restaurant is terrible.
Second diner: Yes, I think it's a case of long time, no sea.

'Mum, now I'm sixteen can I wear lipstick and high heels and have my hair permed?'
'Certainly not, Ralph.'

Oswald couldn't swim, and as he was threshing desperately around in the water his friend Oliver shouted, 'Hey, Oswald, if you don't come up for the third time can I have your bike?'

'There's a man at the door collecting for the children's home's swimming pool.'
'Give him a glass of water.'

What has a bottom at the top?
A leg.

Who wrote A Life on the Ocean Wave?
Eva Lott.

'Doctor, doctor, I'm boiling!'
'Just simmer down, sir.'

When, in frosty midnight,
He cruises through the air,
What Santa needs for Christmas
Is fur-lined underwear.

But when sliding down the chimney
Towards the fire we tend,
Asbestos pants for Santa
Would be better in the end.

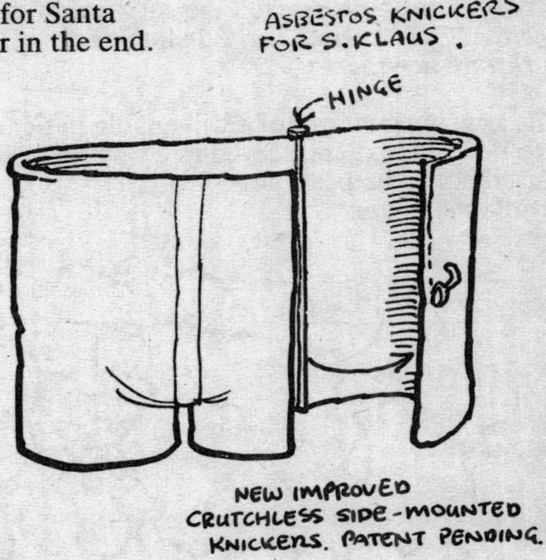

Smart Alec's favourite misprints:

'The bride was very upset when one of the bridesmaids stepped on her brain and tore it.'
Lincolnshire newspaper

'The winners of the competition will be flown to a first-class hotel in Miami, where they will remain for two weeks without having to spend a penny.'
Surrey newspaper

'Mrs Jenkinson discovered the cat dead in the garden, and curried its body indoors.'
Yorkshire newspaper

'The new hospital canteen will enable patients to be prepared and served in a way that used not to be possible.'
Suffolk newspaper

'Strikebound holidaymakers spent over ten hours waiting for the jerry to arrive. When it did it was filled to capacity.'
Dover newspaper

'We note with regret that Colonel Jasper Sturgis is recovering from a road accident.'
Parish newsletter

'Over 500 people took advantage of the mobile clinic and were examined for cancer and other diseases which the clinic offered free of charge.'
Birmingham newspaper

Knock, knock.
Who's there?
Tom Sawyer.
Tom Sawyer who?
Tom Sawyer getting undressed.

Knock, knock.
Who's there?
Thumping.
Thumping who?
Thumping green and slimy just went up your trousers.

Knock, knock.
Who's there?
Stan.
Stan who?
Stan back, I think I'm going to be sick.

What did one casket say to the other casket?
'Is that you coffin?'

'I wouldn't like to say that Elizabeth has big ears, but from the back she looks like the F.A. Cup.'

What's the difference between Margaret Thatcher and polo mints?
People like polos.

Sign in a cannibal's hut: I never met a man I didn't like.

Christopher: Your sister's spoiled, isn't she?
Smart Alec: No, it's just the perfume she wears.

What do you get if you cross a cow with a mule?
Milk with a kick in it.

What do you give an aunt with a sore throat?
Antiseptic.

Kevin: What do you think of Marmaduke?
Keith: I'd like to kick his teeth in, but why should I improve his looks?

Mr Brown: I hate to tell you, but your wife just fell in the wishing well.
Mr Smith: It works!

Knock, knock.
Who's there?
Alec.
Alec who?
Alec most people but I don't like you.

Father: How did the greenhouse get smashed?
Arthur: I was cleaning my catapult and it went off.

Samantha was given a xylophone and a bottle of perfume for her birthday. That evening her parents invited the local vicar and his wife to dinner, and Samantha sat between them. She smiled at them both as they were eating the soup, and confided: 'If you hear a little noise, and smell a little smell, it's me.'

Why is it not safe to sleep on a train?
Because they run over sleepers.

Little Willie from his mirror
Licked the mercury all off,
Thinking, in his childish error,
It would cure his whooping cough.
At the funeral Willie's mother,
Smartly said to Mrs Brown,
' 'Twas a chilly day for Willie when the
mercury went down.'

Len: This restaurant does a good UFO meal.
Ben: What's a UFO meal?
Len: One full of Unidentified Frying Objects.

Clarice: Would you like some nougat?
Veronica: It's pronounced noogar. The T is silent.
Clarice: Not the way you drink it, it isn't!

What did the cannibal say when he saw Santa Claus?
'Goody, goody, Christmas dinner.'

Sharon: I'm so homesick.
Sheila: But this is your home!
Sharon: I know, and I'm sick of it!

What did Lot do with his wife after she turned into a pillar of salt?
Put her in the cellar.

Barry: My new girlfriend's a slick chick!
Harry: You mean she's like a greasy chicken?

Barrister: Your first two wives died when their car brakes failed, and now your third wife has died from food poisoning. It's a bit odd, isn't it?
Prisoner: Not really. She couldn't drive.

Customer: Can I try on those trousers in the window?
Shop assistant: I'm afraid you'll have to use the changing room like everyone else, sir.

Gilly: I throw myself into everything I do.
Milly: Why don't you go and dig a big hole?

What did the Scotsman do when the dentist said he would have to pay £50 to have two teeth out?

He gave the dentist £1 and asked him to loosen them a little.

Knock, knock.
Who's there?
Howard.
Howard who?
Howard you like a punch on the nose?

'Doctor, doctor, I keep thinking I'm a dumpling.'

'Don't get into such a stew.'

What's the definition of a nudist?

Someone who wears a one-button suit.

Knock, knock.
Who's there?
Saul.
Saul who?
Saul over your shoe, you should have looked where you were going.

Doctor: Please breathe in deeply and then take a long breath out.
Patient: Is this so you can check my lungs?
Doctor: No, it's so I can clean my glasses.

Why is it foolish to upset a cannibal?
Because you could find yourself in hot water.

What do cannibals do on Fridays?
Mermaid and chips.

What happened to the dog who lived on garlic?
His bark was worse than his bite.

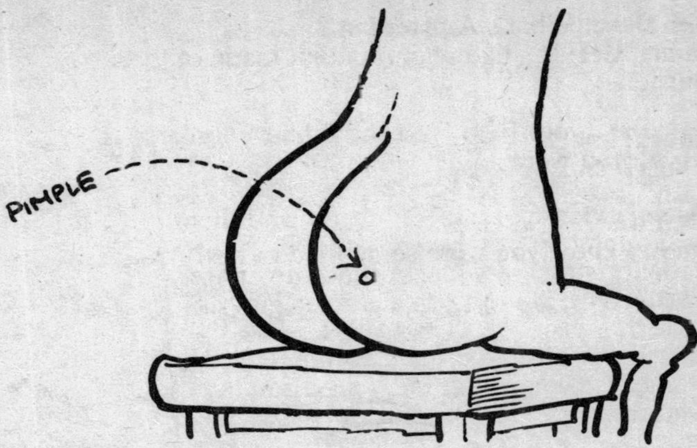

First granny: I've got a new hearing aid.
Second granny: Does it work well?
First granny: The chemist in the High Street.

Colonel Blimp: One of my ancestors died at Waterloo.
Naughty Ned: Really? Which platform?

Did you hear about the disenchanted cannibal?
He'd got fed up with people.

Knock, knock.
Who's there?
Ivor.
Ivor who?
Ivor pimple on my bottom.

Dim Dave: What's Amsterdam?
Smart Alec: It's like plum jam but made of 'amsters.

Knock, knock.
Who's there?
Cash.
Cash who?
I didn't know you were some kind of nut!

I had written to Aunt Maud,
Who was on a trip abroad,
When I heard she'd died of cramp
Just too late to save the stamp.

There was an old woman from China
Who was sent to sea on a liner.
She fell off the deck
And twisted her neck,
And now she can see right behind her.

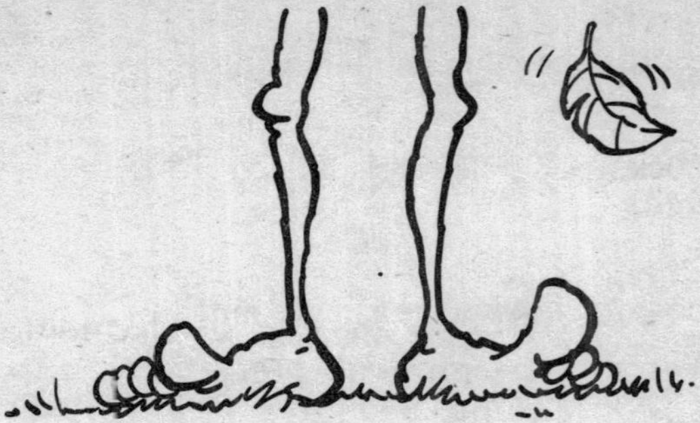

Mr Jones to his son: I don't care if we have got cracks in the ceilings, stop telling your friends you come from a broken home.

What's big, red, and lies upside-down in the gutter?
A dead bus.

Waiter: Would you like some idiot soup?
Diner: What's idiot soup?
Waiter: Thick soup.

Don: Have you ever been to an Adam and Eve party?
Ron: What's an Adam and Eve party?
Don: Leaves off at midnight.

Why did the blind chicken cross the road?
To go to the Bird's Eye shop.

NORA THUD OF NOTTINGHAM
WRITES TO SAY –
"THIS BOOK MAKES ME THROW UP.
IT'S REVOLTING."

YES – IT USUALLY IS NORA –
SAYS OUR EDITOR.

'Waiter, waiter, this egg is bad!'
'Don't blame me, sir, I only laid the table.'

Are you mad if you talk to yourself?
Only if you answer.

First cannibal: Am I late for lunch?
Second cannibal: Yes, everybody's eaten.

Did you hear about the vegetarian cannibal?
He would only eat Swedes.

What does a monster do when he loses his head?
Tries to find a head hunter.

Why did Dracula leave Scunthorpe in a hurry?
Because it was a one-hearse town.

Knock, knock.
Who's there?
Hawaii.
Hawaii who?
I was fine until I met you.

Knock, knock.
Who's there?
Aida.
Aida who?
Aida plateful of prunes and now I've got a stomach ache.

What's the definition of noise?
A skeleton dancing on a tin roof.

What happens when two dozen Irish labourers fall off a roof?
A navvy-lanche.

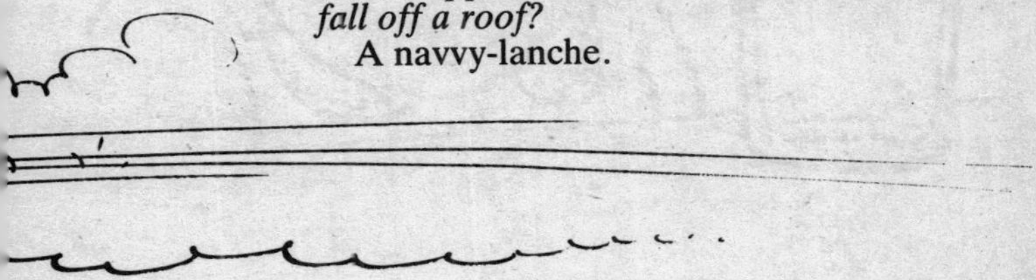

Did you hear about the woman who was so ugly she could make yoghurt by staring at a pint of milk for an hour?

Bert: What's another name for a coffin?
Gert: A snuff box.

Dave: My sister gave her fiancé the push after he'd given her a brass band.
Mave: A brass band?
Dave: Yes. It turned her finger green.

Distraught dentist: But I told you not to swallow! That was my last pair of forceps!

'Is there no hope?' the sick man said.
The doctor silently shook his head,
And took his leave, wtih sighs of sorrow,
Despairing of his fee tomorrow.

There was a young lady of Leeds
Who swallowed ten packets of seeds.
In a month, silly lass,
She was covered in grass
And couldn't sit down for the weeds.

Fred: Who's Nicholas?
Ted: The boy who doesn't wear underwear.

Sign on a chemist's shop: We dispense with accuracy.

Clara: I've just returned from the beauty parlour.
Sarah: Pity it was closed.

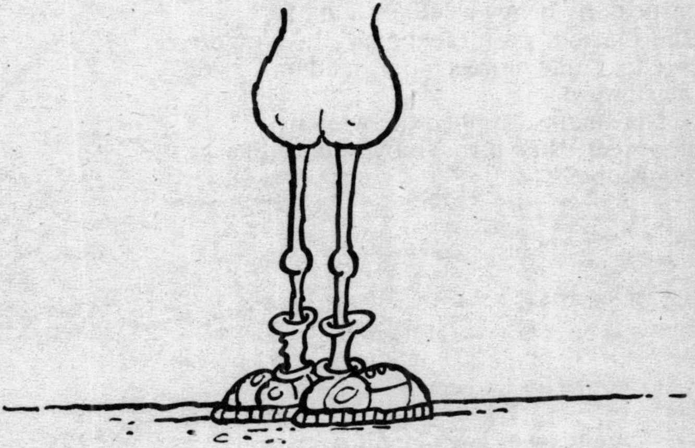

Archimedes: Eureka!
Archimedes' son: What of?
Archimedes: Old plimsolls.

Larry: Our Harry's a real smasher.
Barry: How's that?
Larry: Since he's been doing the washing up we haven't a plate left left in the house!

What's the best thing to put in a pie?
Your teeth.

'Doctor, doctor, I'm boiling!'
'Just simmer down.'

The transatlantic liner was experiencing particularly heavy weather, and Mrs Ramsbottom wasn't feeling well. 'Would you care for some more supper, madam?' asked the steward.

'No, thanks,' replied the wretched passenger. 'Just throw it overboard to save me the trouble.'

Wally: Yesterday I took the first step towards getting divorced.
Olly: Did you see a solicitor?
Wally: No, I got married.

Diner: The celery soup, and then the fish, please waiter.
Waiter: If I were you, sir, I'd have the fish first.
Diner: Why's that?
Waiter: Because it's going bad.

What do you get if you cross a bear with an old pair of socks?
Winnie the Pooh.

What do you get if you cross a Persian carpet with a rhinoceros?
A large pile on the floor.

Gilly: Can I share your skis?
Billy: Of course. We'll go halves with them.
Gilly: That's very kind. Are you sure you don't mind?
Billy: Not at all. I'll have them downhill and you can have them uphill.

'How can I be sure that the buses are running on time?'
'Put your watch in front of one in the road.'

Knock, knock.
Who's there?
Spider.
Spider who?
Spider in the bath when she thought I wasn't looking.

Land of soapy water,
Teacher's having a bath,
Headmaster's looking through the keyhole,
Having a jolly good laugh!

What ancient society does Dracula belong to?
The Consumers' Association.

What's a cannibal's favourite meat?
Grilled chaps.

What is a sadist's favourite soup?
Scream of chicken.

What's black, white and red, and smells?
A skunk with a nappy rash.

Peal: Did you hear about Sid? He fell into a barrel of beer.
Smart Alec: What a bitter end!

Man in street: I'm a stranger here. Where's the nearest boozer?
Second man in street: You're talking to him.

What did the mother herring say to her baby when they saw a submarine?
'Don't worry, it's only a tin of people.'

Class 2B was renowned throughout the school for its noisy and uncontrollable children. Teacher after teacher left in despair. Then one day Mr Barton arrived — and everything changed. The class became quiet and well-behaved, it was quite reasonable. The headmaster made a point of congratulating Mr Barton. 'This is wonderful, Barton,' he said. 'How do you manage to keep 2B on its toes?'
'It's quite simple, sir,' replied Mr Barton. 'I put drawing-pins on their chairs.'

What do you do if you meet a skeleton on a dark night?
Jump out of your skin and say 'Hello'.

What do you call a corpse that rings people's doorbells?
A dead ringer.

What kind of tree does a ghoul plant in its garden?
A ceme-tree.

What does a ghoul like on his dinner?
Grave-y.

What does a vampire like for breakfast?
Ready-neck.

Mr and Mrs Awful were trying very hard to teach their daughter, little Samantha Awful, table manners. 'Don't eat your dinner with your fingers, darling,' said Mrs Awful. 'Use the shovel at the side of your plate.'

Diner: Waiter! This fish pie tastes very funny!
Waiter: Then why aren't you laughing, Sir?

Diner: Waiter! What's this dead cockroach doing in my wine?
Waiter: You asked for something with a little body, sir.

The scout troup had been on a long country ramble, and it was 6 pm before they arrived back at camp. Their leader did a roll-call and discovered that Cuthbert was missing. No one seemed to know where he was. The evening wore on, and the scout leader got more and more worried, until, at 8 pm, he saw young Cuthbert plodding wearily up to his tent.

'Where have you been, Cuthbert?' he asked angrily. 'We've all been very worried about you.'

'Well,' said Cuthbert, 'You remember that field of cows we crossed before we forded the river?'

'Yes,' replied the scout leader.

'Well,' said Cuthbert, 'as we were crossing it my beret blew off, and I had to try on twenty-five before I found the right one.'

Mrs Brown: Who was that at the door?
Veronica: A lady with a baby in a pram.
Mrs Brown: Tell her to push off!

Knock, knock.
Who's there?
Butter.
Butter who?
Butter hurry up, I need to go to the lavatory.

Mary had a little lamb,
It was a greedy glutton.
She fed it on ice-cream all day —
And now it's frozen mutton.

Eeny, meeny, miney, mo.
Sit the baby on the po.
When he's done,
Wipe his bum,
Tell his mother what he's done.

Why did the chicken cross the road?
To prove that it had guts.

'Mummy, mummy, there's a man at the door with a nasty look on his face!'

'Tell him you've already got one.'

Mrs Jones was trapped on the fourteenth floor of a burning block of flats with her baby. A fireman told her to throw the baby down to him, but she refused. 'It's all right, madam,' he said, 'I can catch. I'm the best goalkeeper the local football team has.'

So Mrs Jones threw down her baby. The fireman caught it, gave it a bounce, and kicked it over the wall.

'Is it wrong to play football on a Sunday, vicar?'

'The way you play it it's a sin on any day.'

'Doctor, doctor, I feel like an old sock!'

'Darn me, I thought there was a funny smell in here.'

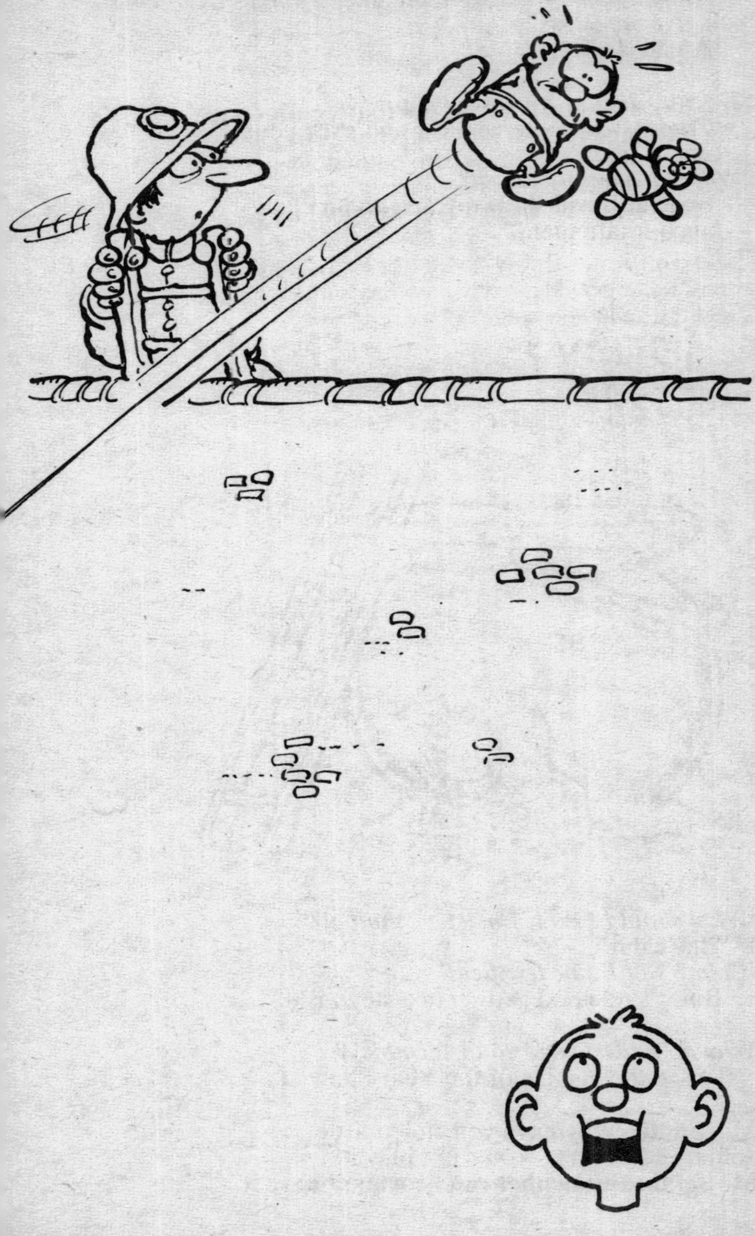

'Doctor, doctor, what would it take to make you give me a kiss?'
'An anaesthetic.'

'Doctor, doctor, my throat is sore.'
'Come over to the window and stick your tongue out.'
'Will that cure my throat?'
'No, but it will show my neighbours how much I hate them.'

'What should I do if I meet a cannibal?'
'Stay calm.'
'Calm? But I'd be terrified!'
'But it's no good getting in a stew, is it?'

Why do undertakers go to Wembley?
To see the Hearse of the Year Show.

Mrs Smith: Why have you stolen little Johnny's trumpet? You can't play it.
Mr Smith: But neither can he while I have it.

What did the idiot call his pet zebra?
Spot.

Jim: Where are you rushing off to?
Tim: To the hospital. I don't like the look of my wife.
Jim: Can I come with you? I can't stand the sight of mine!

Mrs Sidebottom: Did you know most accidents happen in the kitchen?
Mr Sidebottom: Yes. I have to eat them.

Thought for the day: Every dog has his day, but only a dog with a broken tail has a weak end.

What was the Irish cannibal's favourite soup?
A broth of a boy.

What musical instrument does a skeleton play?
A trom-bone.

Mrs Clara Custard was on trial for murdering her husband. The trial had lasted for several days, as there were lots of complications, but finally she was found guilty. Before passing sentence, the judge gave her a puzzled look, and said, 'After what I've heard, Mrs Custard, I can understand why you wanted to get rid of your husband. But why did you shoot him with a bow and arrow?'

'I didn't want to wake the baby,' explained Mrs Custard.

Ollie: Did you hear about Paddy Finnegan's wife?
Dolly: No, what about her?
Ollie: She's so ugly that when they got married everybody kissed him.

Sign in a cafe: All drinking water in this establishment has been personally passed by the manager.

Why do traffic wardens wear hats with yellow bands around them?
So people don't park on their heads.

Teacher: Have you heard about the man in the moon, Alec?
Smart Alec: Yes, miss, but he's not as interesting as the girl in the *Sun*.

Knock, knock.
Who's there?
Muscat.
Muscat who?
Muscat to the loo before I wet my pants.

'Quick! Pass me that hammer! There's a fly on the baby's head!

First cannibal: I don't know what to make of my new secretary.
Second cannibal: How about mincemeat?

Woman in pub: Do you do the pools?
Man in pub: No, it's my dog. He's not house-trained.

Did you hear about the dog that has no legs and is called Marlboro? His master takes him out for a drag.

Did you hear about the man who was so stupid that when he picked his nose he tore the lining of his hat?

Sign in a launderette: Those using automatic washers should remove their clothes when the lights go out.

'Waiter! Waiter! There's a hand in my soup!'
'That's not your soup, sir, that's a fingerbowl.'

'Mummy, mummy, why do you keep poking daddy in the ribs?'
'If I don't the fire will go out.'

What do vampires eat with bread and cheese?
Pickled organs.

Why did the elephant cross the road?
To pick up the flattened chicken.

What's the best way to use a hammer?
Get someone else to hold the nails.

Magnificent mistakes:

The new bride is approximately 75 feet wide from buttress to buttress.

Husbands and children were included in last Wednesday's Women's Institute pot luck supper.

The collection included specimens of local insects protected by special drawers.

If the baby does not thrive on cold milk, boil it.

Passengers complain: many were hit by cancelled trains.

Mr Biggins is a retarded old gentleman on a pension.

For Sale: 1946 Mercedes hearse. Good condition. Original body.

Save time and cut fingers with our new multi-blade chopper.

Mrs Jones said she thought she recognised the man, because his head looked just like her husband's behind.

A very nourishing broth can be made of the remains if there is someone unwell in the house.

Old Mr Kelly
Had a pimple on his belly.
His wife cut it off
And it tasted just like jelly.

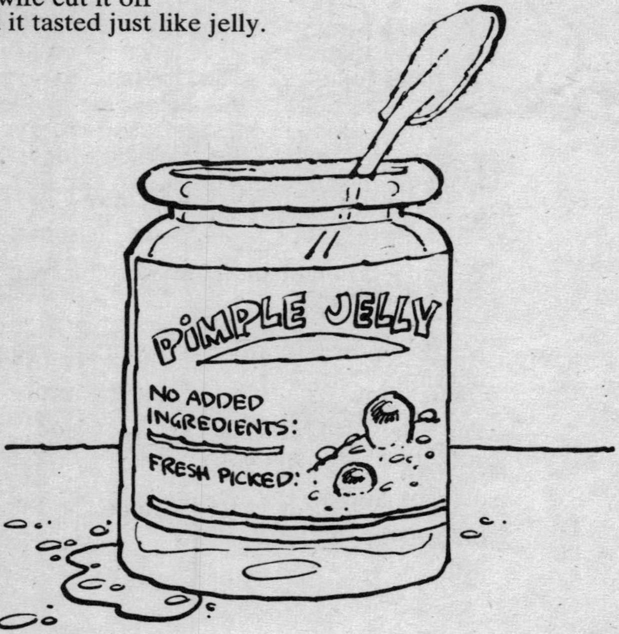

One, two, three,
Me mother caught a flea,
Put it in the teapot
To make a cup of tea.

Bert: My dog's bone idle.
Gert: Why's that?
Bert: When I water the garden he never lifts a leg to help me.

Did you hear about the stupid dog that ate its bone lying down? When it stood up it only had three legs.

Mrs Smith went to the supermarket and tied up her Alsatian outside. A few moments later Mrs Jones followed her in, having tied up her Yorkshire terrier outside. Mrs Jones had less shopping to do than Mrs Smith, so she went back to her dog first. But she'd no sooner got outside than she rushed back into the shop, saying, 'Whose is that Alsatian outside?'

'It's mine,' replied Mrs Smith. 'Is something wrong?'

'I'm afraid it is,' said Mrs Jones. 'My dog has just killed yours.'

'But that's impossible,' said Mrs Smith. 'Mine is a large Alsatian, it would take a huge dog to kill it. What kind of dog is yours?'

'A Yorkshire terrier,' replied Mrs Jones.

'But how could a Yorkshire terrier kill an Alsatian?' asked Mrs Smith.

'It got stuck in the Alsatian's throat and he choked to death,' explained Mrs Jones.

What did Mrs Werewolf say to Mr Werewolf?
'The baby's howling again.'

Cry, baby, cry,
Punch him in the eye,
Hang him on the lamp post
And leave him there to dry.

Jennifer: Do you like my new hairstyle?
Veronica: In as much as it covers half your face, yes.

The rain makes everything beautiful,
It makes the flowers blue.
If the rain makes everything beautiful,
Why doesn't it rain on you?

Overheard on Christmas Eve: 'I don't care who you are, you great fat oaf, get those reindeer off my roof!'

What do you call a man with a 20-ton crane on his head?
Dead.

Admiring Arthur: You really do catch everybody's eye, you know.
Sweet Sue: I know. I use them to play marbles.

First stage cannibal: I say, I say, I say, who was that lady I saw you with last night?
Second stage cannibal: That was no lady, that was tomorrow's dinner.

'Mummy, mummy, I hate my brother's guts!'
'Be quiet and eat what's on your plate.'

Sign in a monster's sitting room: Home is where you hang your head.

Mrs Creepy: Did you like the tongue salad, dear?
Mr Creepy: It spoke for itself, darling.

What did the monster cannibal say when it saw the 7.15 from Britain packed with commuters?
'Goody, goody, a chew-chew train.'

What did the headless horseman say when he woke up?
'Oh dear, I must have nodded off.'

How can you stop a cold in the nose going to your chest?
By tying a knot in your neck.

'Doctor, doctor, do the tests show that I'm quite normal?'

'Yes, Mr James, both your heads are quite all right.'

Smart Alec: What is that terrible, ugly thing on your shoulders?
Silly Sally: Help! What is it?
Smart Alec: Your head.

Knock, knock.
Who's there?
Justin.
Justin who?
Justin in time for a punch in the face.

Knock, knock.
Who's there?
Pudding.
Pudding who?
Pudding your trousers on before your knickers is not a good idea.

Very large man getting out of taxi: You drove here very slowly, driver.
Taxi driver: Yes, sir, but now you've got out I'll be able to go a lot faster.

Nellie: I'm so unpopular no one will talk to me at school.
Kelly: That's nothing. I'm so unpopular the phone doesn't ring even when I'm in the bath.
Melly: You two should talk. I'm so unhappy I'm going to leave home when we get one.

'Daddy, daddy, can I have another glass of water, please?'

'But that's the tenth one I've given you tonight!'

'Yes, but the baby's bedroom's still on fire!'

'Mum, are the Higginbottoms very poor people?'

'I don't think so, Jimmy. Why do you ask?'

'Because they made such a fuss when their baby swallowed a ten-pence piece.'

First cannibal: I don't like my mother-in-law.
Second cannibal: I don't like her much, either. Let's try a bit more salt and pepper.

'My mother-in-law's a real treasure. I wish she was buried treasure.'

Did you hear about the stupid boy who shot both his parents so he could go on the orphans' seaside outing?

Bertha: What's your favourite party game?
Bertie: Pinning the tail on the donkey.
Bertha: I bet you have a sore ass for weeks afterwards.

Did you hear about the Irish boy who had a soft spot for his maths teacher? It was a bog in the middle of Ireland.

Knock, knock.
Who's there?
Warren.
Warren who?
Warren my birthday suit today.

'Doctor, doctor, I feel terribly run down.'
'I'm not surprised, there are tyre marks all over your chest.'

What did the vampire say to the estate agent?
'I don't want a very large house, just somewhere I can string a few people up.'

What's a vampire's favourite lunch?
Baked beings on toast.

What did the lamb chop say as it was about to be put on a skewer?
'Spear me, spear me!'

Why did Desmond the dunce hit the happy fortune teller across the face?
Because he'd always been told to strike a happy medium.

Mrs Arbuthnot: Have you put the cat out, Henry?
Mr Arbuthnot: I didn't even know it was on fire.

Horace: Grandma fell down the steps last week.
Humphrey: Cellar?
Horace: No, I think she can be repaired.

Smart Alec: What does T E R R I F Y spell?
Dumb Dora: Terrify.
Smart Alec: Right. And what does T I S S U E spell?
Dumb Dora: Tissue.
Smart Alec: Right again. Now put them together.
Dumb Dora: Terrify tissue?
Smart Alec: Not at all, go ahead!

'Doctor, doctor, I keep thinking I'm a canary!'
'I can't tweet you, go and see a vet.'

'Doctor, doctor, I'm nervous, this is the first brain operation I've had.'
'Don't worry, it's the first I've ever performed.'

How do you raise a baby monster that's been orphaned?
With a fork-lift truck.

The baker's wife, Selina Smith,
Had lots and lots of fun,
For every time she did her hair
She put it in a bun.

Quick, quick, the cat's been sick.
Where? Where? Under the chair.
Hasten, hasten, fetch the basin.
No, no, fetch the po.
Kate, Kate, you're far too late,
The carpet's in a dreadful state.

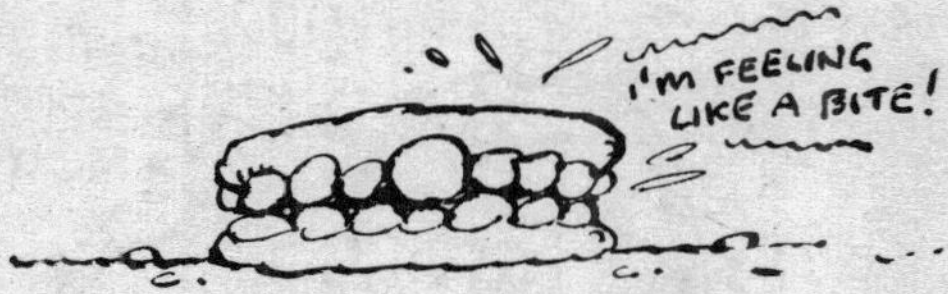

Sandy: We've just got a new dog. Would you like to come and see him?
Andy: Does he bite?
Sandy: That's what I'm trying to find out.

Two fleas were sitting on Robinson Crusoe's back as he lay on the beach on the sun. 'Well, so long,' said one to the other. 'I'll see you on Friday.'

Samantha, visiting Aunty in hospital: I've brought you a box of your favourite chocolates.
Aunty: Oh, good! But the box is almost empty!
Samantha: They're my favourites, too.

Mrs Crocodile: My husband wears my photograph over his heart. It saved his life once, when a burglar tried to shoot him.
Mrs Alligator: I'm not surprised. Your face would stop anything.

What happened when Desmond the dunce went to a mind-reader?
She gave him his money back.

Why did Desmond the dunce eat little pieces of metal all day long?
Because he'd heard about a staple diet.

Cannibal butcher: Do you prefer your meat grilled or fried?
His wife: Oh, do stop talking chop!

What's yellow, brown and hairy?
Cheese on toast dropped on the carpet.

'Waiter! There's a bluebottle in my soup!'
'Yes, sir, there's a police station round the corner.'

Baby skunk: May I have a chemistry set for Christmas?
Mother skunk: What? And stink the house out?

A man arrived at a seaside hotel where he had made a reservation rather late at night. All the lights were out, so he knocked on the door. After a long time a light appeared in an upstairs window and a woman called out, 'Who are you? What do you want?'

'I'm John Jackson,' he called. 'I'm staying here.'

'Stay there, then,' she retorted, and slammed the window shut.

Hettie: I've changed my mind.
Betty: Oh, good. Does it work better than the old one?

Mr Jones: You can take your thumb out of the leaking pipe now, son.
Little Johnny: Hooray! Has the plumber come?
Mr Jones: No, but the house is on fire.

Mr Priddle: I think I'm dying, Prunella.
Mrs Priddle: I think you are, Percy dear.
Mr Priddle: May I have one last request?
Mrs Priddle: Of course. What is it?
Mr Priddle: May I have a piece of that special iced cake you made?
Mrs Priddle: Certainly not! I'm saving that for your funeral!

Hickory, dickory, dock.
Three mice ran up the clock.
The clock struck one —
The rest ran away.

'Dad, that Mr Jenkins down the road said you weren't fit to live with pigs!'
'What did you say, son?'
'I stuck up for you. I said you were certainly fit to live with pigs.'

Notice on the town hall board: Due to the current strike of council workers, people are advised not to die, as grave-digging can only be carried out by a skeleton team.

THANKS TO MR. HENRY LIGHTS OF LIVERPOOL FOR THIS LAST JOKE.

LETS HOPE THE GRAVE-DIGGERS AREN'T BONE IDLE EH - LIGHTS?

EDITOR.

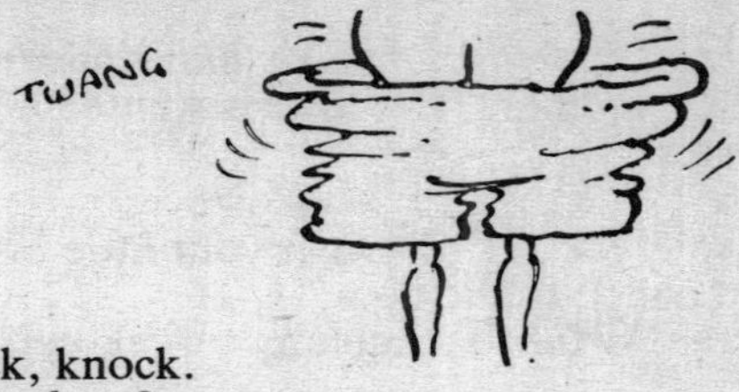

Knock, knock.
Who's there?
Pencil
Pencil who?
Pencil fall down if the elastic breaks.

First ghoul: You look tired out.
Second ghoul: I am. I'm dead on my feet.

Little boy kneels at the foot of the bed,
Dirty great lump on the top of his head,
Hush, hush, whisper who dares,
Christopher Robin has fallen downstairs.

Colonel Blimp: That's a mighty fine stuffed lion!
The Honourable Blump: My father bagged it when he went on safari with Lord Lovaduck.
Colonel Blimp: What's it stuffed with?
The Honourable Blump: Lord Lovaduck.

What did the cannibal say after he'd eaten the TV comic?
'I've got a very funny feeling in the pit of my stomach!'

'Jeremy! Put down that axe immediately!'
'But, mummy, I've always wanted a half-sister!'

Nervous guest: But *why* is your little brother's head nailed to the floor?
Darren Awful: It's mummy's week-end treat.

KOMPETITION CORNER

YES FANS – SEND IN YOUR HORRIBLE YUCKY DRAWING OF YOUR PET HAMSTER BEING ICKY ON GRANS HEARING AID. THE LUCKY WINNER WILL WIN A HOLS FOR SIXTY TO A FAR OFF DESERT ISLAND.

ANSWERS TO :–
"HEAVE ON GRAN,"
PO BOX 392, LONDON WC936 67PU!
AND ENCLOSE A STAMPED ADDRESSED SOCK.

Smart Alec: Did you hear about the werewolf who appeared on a TV comedy show?
Dim Dinah: No. What about him?
Smart Alec: He had the audience howling with laughter.

Sally: Mum, there's a huge black cat in the garden.
Mum: That's all right. Black cats are lucky.
Sally: This one isn't. It's just eaten Rover.

Little Kevin Klever-klogs was showing off his new BMX bike to his friends. Round and round he rode, shouting out as he whizzed past them, 'Look, no hands! Look, no feet! Oops! Look, no teeth!'

There was a fierce chief of the Sioux
Who into a gun barrel blioux
To see if 'twas loaded;
The rifle exploded —
As he should have known it would dioux!

A pilot flying over the jungle was having trouble with his plane and decided to bail out before it crashed. So he got into his parachute, jumped, pulled the rip-cord, and drifted gently down to land. Unfortunately he landed right in a large cooking pot which a tribal chief was simmering gently over a fire.

The chief looked at him, rubbed his eyes, looked again, and asked, 'What's this flier doing in my soup?'

Mrs Snooty: You will have to teach your puppy manners. He's just bitten my ankle.
Mrs Fruity: That's because he's not yet big enough to bite your neck.

What do you get if you cross a vampire with the Abominable Snowman?
Frostbite.

IT'S EVEN BETTER IN COLOUR FOLKS!

'Well done, Mrs Carruthers. You have just won first prize in our pull-an-ugly-face contest.'
'But I didn't even enter!'

What's a sea monster's favourite supper?
Fish and ships.

Magnificent mistakes:

The Women's Institute talk on Wednesday will be about wild flowers in gardens, and Mrs Carrington-Smythe will show slides of her beautiful wild pants.

Advertisement for a Chinese takeaway:
Authentic Chinese food. Eat now — bring back later if not satisfied.

Advertisement for an Indian restaurant: Genuine hot, strong curries. All our customers are regular.

Young lady seeks two days a week housework — or would divide in two.

Room to let, suitable for two young ladies, use of kitchen or two gentlemen.

Order your ring by post. State size or enclose string tied round finger.

Pedigree Labrador puppies for sale. Sire: Champion Satterthwaite Samson. Dam well bred.

FARMER SAVED AFTER TEN-HOUR VIGIL IN BOG.

NEW POISON THREAT AFTER MINISTER HEADS FOR BEACH.

POLICE OFFICER CONVICTED FOR ACCEPTING BRIDE.

MAN GIVEN LIFE FOR KILLING WIFE BEFORE MOTHER.

For sale: Three-bra electric firc.

Young lady required for insurance office, previous experience, not essential bust, be able to type.

For sale: Three-bedroomed house, dining-room, lounge, kitchen, bathroom, sep. W.C. three miles Wolverhampton.

If you shoot yourself and have not used Jenkinson's Cartridges you have missed one of the good things in life.

The Village Society ladies held a 'Swap Afternoon' on Saturday. Everybody brought something they didn't want. Many were accompanied by their husbands.

To help Greenbury's new young football team, a local sports shop has kindly donated 20 tracksuit tops and ten bottoms.

One of the prime requirements of a boy scout is to be able to cook himself.

For sale: Surgical instruments, good assortment of deceased surgeons.

Does your raincoat let in water? Use our Super Spray — it will ensure it is really repellent.

Next season's range contains many shoes for girls with low-cut fancy uppers.

Have your children photographed at the convenience of your own home.

* HURRY UP YOU OLD TWERP – THIS SEAT'S COLD!

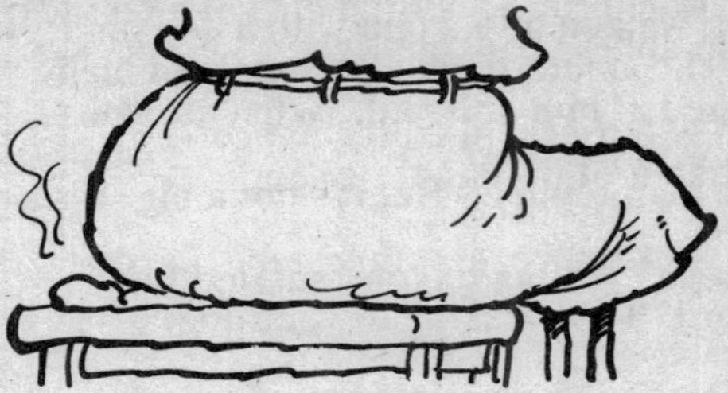

I love you, I love you,
Be my valentine.
And give me your bubble gum —
You're sitting on mine.

Mildred, at cinema: I love you so much I've got a cold, slithery feeling down my neck.
Mervyn, her boyfriend: So that's where my ice-cream went!

Harriet: I must go now. Don't bother to see me to the door.
Harold: It's no bother. It's a pleasure.

Mr Jones: I think my wife should have been born in the Dark Ages.
Mr Smith: Why's that?
Mr Jones: She looks terrible in a bright light.

Sally: My brother's written a novel to be published after he's dead.
Susie: I can't wait to read it.

A man walked into a pub with a dog on a lead. The landlord, an evil-tempered man, glowered at him and said, 'What are you doing with that pig?'

The man replied, 'But it's not a pig. It's a dog.'

'I wasn't talking to you,' snarled the landlord. 'I was talking to your dog.'

Teacher: Do you know what a guillotine is?
Smart Alec: Something that gives you a pain in the neck.

'Doctor, doctor, I've got a bad liver. What should I do?'

'Take it back to the butcher.'

What happened when Rover ran off with some of a skeleton's bones?

He didn't have a leg to stand on.

What's the difference between a dog and a flea?

A dog can have fleas but a flea can't have dogs.

'My dog has no tail.'

How do you tell when he's happy?'

'He stops biting me.'

Dim Dinah: What happened to your grandfather?
Smart Alec: He disappeared on a deep-sea diving trip.
Dim Dinah: Oh dear, what happened?
Smart Alec: Something he disagreed with ate him.

Swimmer: Help! A shark's just bitten off my foot!
Friend: Which one?
Swimmer: How should I know? All sharks look alike to me.

What happened when the idiot had a brain transplant?

The brain rejected him.

'Doctor, doctor, help me! My throat's like a furred-up pipe!'
'Then go and see a plumber.'

Who hit J.R. with a tomahawk?
Sioux Ellen.

What kind of bandage do people wear after heart surgery?
Ticker tape.

An insurance salesman called on Mrs Brown. 'You really should have life insurance. If your husband were to die, what would you get?'
Mrs Brown pondered for a few moments. 'I think I'd get a parrot. Then the house wouldn't seem so quiet.'

Mrs Jones: Did the music teacher really say your voice was heavenly?
Little Jenny: Well, not exactly in those words. She said it was like nothing on earth.

Mr Smith: I want you to bury my wife.
Undertaker: But I buried your wife last year, sir.
Mr Smith: I remarried.
Undertaker: Congratulations, sir.

Mrs Sidebottom: And what will you have to follow the pie, dear?
Mr Sidebottom: Indigestion, as usual, I expect.

How many skunks does it take to make a big stink?
A phew.

What do you do if you split your sides laughing?
Run until you get a stitch.

Two shipwrecked sailors managed to climb onto an iceberg. 'Oh, dear,' said the first, 'do you think we'll survive?'

'Of course we will,' said the second. 'Look, here comes the *Titanic*.'

What airline do vampires travel on?

British Scareways.

Mr and Mrs Blenkinsop were always fighting. Then one morning as Mrs Blenkinsop was going to the launderette she was knocked down by a hit and run driver. A policeman rushed up and asked her if she'd taken the car's number.

'I didn't need to,' replied Mrs Blenkinsop. 'It was my husband in that car.'

'Did you see him?' asked the policeman.

'No,' said Mrs Blenkinsop, 'but I'd know that laugh anywhere.'

Last night I slew my wife,
Stretched her out on the parquet flooring.
I was loath to take her life,
But I had to stop her snoring.

What happened when two very fat men fell off Beachy Head?
Boom! Boom!

Knock, knock.
Who's there?
Gopher.
Gopher who?
Gopher a walk over the cliff.

What was the old drunkard's final drink?
His bier.

Doctor to balding patient: I'm afraid I can't give you anything to grow more hair on your head. But I could shrink your head to fit the hair you've already got.

Teacher: What's the most important thing to remember in a chemistry lesson?
Smart Alec: Not to lick the spoon.

What do you get if you sit under a cow?
A pat on the head.

Why did the one-handed man cross the road?
To get to the secondhand shop.

How can you tell an old person from a young person?
An old person can sing and brush their teeth at the same time.

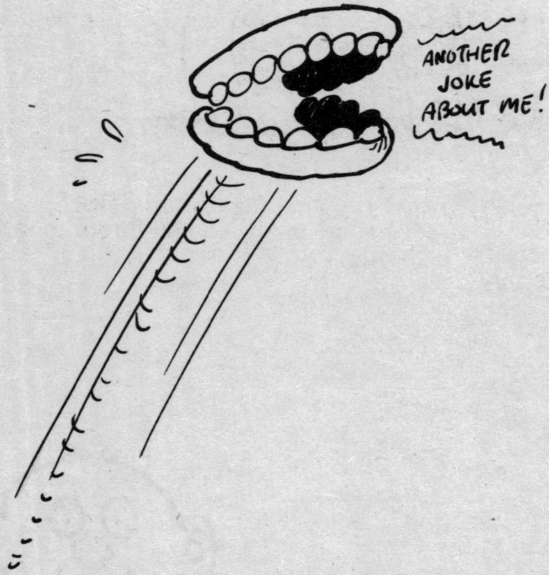

Why was the skeleton unhappy at the Hallowe'en dance?
Because he had nobody to dance with.

What do you get if you cross a vampire with a telescope?
A horrorscope.

How do you get a paper baby?
Marry an old bag.

'Why are you jumping up and down?'
'I took some medicine and forgot to shake the bottle.'

What did the mother biscuit say as her son crossed the road?
'Oh, crumbs!'

First snake: Are we supposed to be poisonous?
Second snake: Why?
First snake: I just bit my lip.

Did you hear about the karate expert who joined the army? The first time he saluted he nearly killed himself.

What does Dracula drink at breakfast time?
Blood orange juice.

What's the underneath of a graveyard called?
The spirit level.

If you like grave humour, I might tell you the story of the body snatchers. On second thoughts, I won't. You might get carried away.

Science teacher: What are bacteria?
Smart Alec: The rear entrances to cafeterias.

First burglar: Quick! It's the police! Jump out of the window!
Second burglar: But we're on the thirteenth floor!
First burglar: This is no time to be superstitious.

A dog called June was always picking fights with larger animals. One day she had an argument with a lion. The next day was the first of July. Why?
Because that was the end of June!

How do fleas travel from place to place?
By itch hiking.

What would you do if you saw six vampires walking down the road?
Hope they were going to a fancy dress party.

What's a vampire's favourite song?
'Fangs for the Memory.'

If a lion ate the prime minister, what time would it be?
8 p.m. (ate P.M.).

Preserve wildlife — pickle a hedgehog today.

What's the different between a nail and a boxer?
One gets knocked in, the other gets knocked out.

What goes in pink and comes out blue?
A swimmer in January.

Knock, knock.
Who's there?
Ahab.
Ahab who?
Ahab to go to the loo in a hurry!

Two old friends met for the first time in twenty years. 'How's life been for you?' asked the first man.

'Not too good,' replied the second. 'My first wife died, my second wife left me, my son's in prison, my daughter was run over by a bus, my house was hit by a low-flying aircraft, my pet dog has distemper, and the doctor thinks I'm suffering from an incurable disease.'

'Oh, dear,' said the first man. 'That does sound bad. What business are you in?'

'I sell lucky charms,' said the first man sadly.

There was an old man of Vancouver
Whose wife got sucked up by the hoover.
He said, 'There's some doubt
If she's more in than out,
But whichever it is I can't move her.'

Smith Minor, whose first name was Paul,
Narrowly missed a bad fall —
He broke several teeth
And the jawbone beneath,
Seven ribs, and a leg, but that's all.

Knock, knock.
Who's there?
Moppet.
Moppet who?
Moppet up quickly before someone treads in it.

'Mummy, mummy, the pet lion's just bitten off my foot!'

'Well, keep out of the kitchen until it stops bleeding. I've just washed the floor.'

What did the boy maggot say to the girl maggot?
'What's a nice girl like you doing in a joint like this?'

And, finally, a collection of epitaphs and rhymes about some ill-fated people.

Little Willie's dead
Shove him in a coffin
'Cos you don't get chance
Of a funeral often!

This stone was erected in memory of Patrick O'Malley
Drowned in the River Liffey
By a few kind friends

Here lies Hannah Anderson, 1823-1866
Let her R.I.P.

Beneath this stone, a lump of clay,
Lies Uncle Peter Daniels,
Who early in the month of May
Took off his winter flannels.

Ebenezer Johnson
Was buried here on 18 December 1821
By the desire of his wife
Alice Johnson.

Here lies a chump who got no gain
By jumping from a moving train.
Banana skins on platform seven
Ensured his terminus was heaven.

It wasn't the cough that carried him off,
It was the coffin they carried him off in.

The manner of her death was thus —
She was druv over by a bus.

Here lies the body of Michael Shay
Who died maintaining his right of way.
His case was clear and his will was strong —
But he's as dead as if he'd been wrong.

John Makepeace said that his car couldn't
skid —
This monument shows that it could, and did.

Little Willie,
Pair of skates,
Hole in ice —
Pearly gates.

Here lies the body of Samuel Jenkins
Who gallantly gave up his life
To save a perishing lady.

On a dentist

Stranger! Approach this spot with gravity
John Brown is filling his last cavity.

On a munitions worker

The bomb he had went off too soon,
And here his story ceases.
The parts they found are buried here —
And thus he Rests in Pieces.